A Bibliography
of
Psychohistory

Garland Reference Library of Social Science (Vol. 6)

A Bibliography
of
Psychohistory

edited by
Lloyd deMause

Garland Publishing, Inc., New York & London

1975

Library of Congress Cataloging in Publication Data
Main entry under title:

A Bibliography of psychohistory.

(Garland reference library in social science ; v. 6)
    1. Psychohistory--Bibliography. I. DeMause, Lloyd.
Z6208.M5D45 [D16]   016.155   75-5140
ISBN 0-8240-9999-0

CONTENTS

FOREWORD

LLOYD
deMAUSE

One is not often privileged to be present at the birth of a new discipline. The nineteenth century seems at times to have had a monopoly on new departures—sociology, anthropology and even modern psychology have all been invented in the nineteenth century. Only psychoanalysis barely makes it into the twentieth century, the official publication date of Freud's *Interpretation of Dreams* having been 1900, although it actually was printed in 1899. Yet for the past three-quarters of a century, during which time the physical sciences have initiated dozens of new disciplines, the human sciences have been content to develop along the lines laid down a century or more earlier in each of their fields. The current academic scholasticism and overspecialization is perhaps more a result of this absence of new beginnings than of anything else.

A few years ago, however, it became evident to many that a completely new discipline was about to be born—psychohistory. Just as sociology had its roots in many older disciplines, ultimately reaching back to the Greeks, so psychohistory has its roots in what used to be called "applied psychoanalysis," in certain trends in historical writing, in social psychology, and so on. In fact, many of the entries listed in this Bibliography are more in the nature of anticipations than they are examples of modern psychohistory. The word itself, in its earlier hyphenated version, simply meant "applying psychology to history," although even then it was usually psychoanalytic psychology that was being "applied." With the founding in 1973 of the new scholarly journal, *History of Childhood Quarterly: The Journal of Psychohistory,* this definition was expanded to envision psychohistory as a complete "history of the psyche." Psychohistory had become a new *science of patterns of historical motivations,* less a division of history or psychology than a replacement for sociology, based on a set of problems, a conscious methodology and criteria of excellence all its own.

Several converging developments in intellectual history have been responsible for the new departure taking place now. The first was the discovery that the history of childhood followed evolutionary patterns that were lawful, and that the differing childhoods found in history could be an empirical basis for studying the changing personality patterns of individuals and groups in history. The second was the development of psychoanalytic small-group process theory, which during the 1960's began, for the first time, to provide useful paradigms for extending clinical psychoanalytic insight into larger groups by identifying group fantasies, group defenses, and other shared needs on a strictly empirical basis while avoiding the holistic reification of "society" which underlies both sociology and anthropology.

The third development was a new attitude of radical empiricism in psychohistory. In "applied psychoanalysis" the central methodology was to describe historical character, either of "great men" or of whole nations, to apply clinical psychoanalytic categories to the character-type, and to infer—which is to say, make an educated guess at—the underlying childhood experiences which clinical practice led the psychoanalyst to believe had formed the adult character. Often the guesses were accurate enough, just as often they were wide of the mark, but the main methodological point was that right or wrong they were uncorrectable because they were only inferences. One could find in history only what one found on the couch. And so it was determined that Napoleon had had an Oedipus complex, that Hitler had witnessed a primal scene, and that Russia was expansionist because Russians had been swaddled. The first of these was true but trivial, the second doubtful and unprovable, and the third completely false. None contributed to the development of a science of psychohistory.

What the new psychohistorians are creating is a radical empiricism which moves from actual evidence of childhood and adolescent experience to actual evidence of adult motivational patterns, each discovered only through painstaking historical research into the primary documentation. The results contain that element of *surprise* which is the mark of true discovery, not only surprise in terms of the unsuspected connections between childhood and shared adult motivations in history but also surprise in the sense that psychohistory is contributing to the revision and extension of psychoanalytic psychology itself. This is possible because only psychohistory can work forward in time as well as backwards, because it has a wealth of historical material available for discovery and confirmation of connections unavailable to the psychotherapist, who can only observe a few years of one life at a time.

The new psychohistory works on three levels, sometimes all three within the same piece of research but theoretically distinguishable. They are all concerned with historical motivation, but are quite separate from the discipline of history. These three levels are: (1) the history of childhood, (2) psychobiography, and (3) group psychohistory.

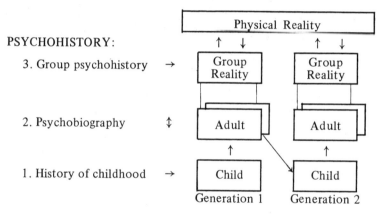

Two things can be noted from this paradigm for psychohistory. First, psychohistorians, in their intense concentration on psychic reality, must pretty much leave the determination of the physical reality of history to traditional historians. If one spends one's life searching for evidence of the complexities of motivations behind the Christian impulse to go on Crusades, one must trust the narrative historian's description of how they got there, which battles were fought, who won what, and all the other physical details of the Crusades. Similarly, it continues to be the province of the historian to detail whether Germany in 1939 did in fact suffer from overpopulation; but whether it did or not, it is the province of the psychohistorian alone to determine whether the desire for *Lebensraum* and the resulting political action did *in fact* come from population pressure or from other sources. The psychohistorian claims the field of historical motivation as his or her own specialty, and further claims that only psychohistorical evidence as presented by a qualified psychohistorian, *according to the criteria of the science of psychohistory,* can determine historical motivation—limited only by the general rule that any science is open to corroboration by others.

Secondly, psychohistory as a separate discipline is just beginning to produce its own literature, its own associations, its own courses, its own criteria of excellence. The historical situation today is much the same as when psychology separated from philosophy or sociology from economics in the latter half of the nineteenth century. Because of this fact, the following Bibliographic Guide is an invaluable research tool. It will enable teachers of courses in psychohistory and the history of childhood to prepare reading lists, scholars to locate previous psychohistorical research and theoretical discussions, and the field in general to determine where its strengths—and weaknesses—lie at this early stage of its development.

Psychohistory is currently being taught and practiced by scholars who were originally formally trained in history, education, political science, psychology, psychoanalysis, psychiatry, sociology, the humanities; indeed almost every academic and mental health discipline has contributed to the new science. Courses in psychohistory are now being taught in many different academic departments—often jointly, for instance by both a psychoanalyst and a historian—and are even being included in the curricula of psychotherapeutic training centers. If this Bibliographic Guide should assist this wide range of scholars in their task of founding their new discipline, it will have performed its function, and those of us who worked together to prepare it will feel that we have contributed to an exciting moment in intellectual history.

A Bibliography
of Psychohistory

FAYE
SINOFSKY,
JOHN J.
FITZPATRICK,
LOUIS W.
POTTS, and
LLOYD
deMAUSE

This bibliography is designed to aid historians, psychiatrists, psycho-analysts, political psychologists, sociologists, educators and others interested in the literature and sources of the new discipline of psychohistory. The net has been cast widely—citations include journal articles, books, unpublished papers and doctoral dissertations. Psychohistory has been broadly defined as the use of modern psychology in interpreting history. Thus the entries range from the development of theoretical models to their application in the studies of childhood, shared themes, mass behavior and leadership as well as other facets of psychohistory. Psychoanalytic studies of purely literary and of anthropological material have not been included. In order to assist students and others in constructing courses in psychohistory, items of more than usual interest have been marked with an asterisk (*). The bibliography is by author within six sections:

I. Methodology and General   IV. Medieval and Renaissance
II. History of Childhood   V. Modern
III. Ancient   VI. Asia

1

I. METHODOLOGY AND GENERAL

Abell, Walter. *The Collective Dream in Art: A Psycho-historical Theory of Culture Based on Relations Between the Arts, Psychology, and the Social Sciences.* Cambridge, Mass.: Harvard University Press, 1957.

Abraham, Karl. "Observations of the Cult of the Mother and its Symbolism in Individual and Folk Psychology." In his *Clinical Papers and Essays on Psychoanalysis.* New York: Basic Books, 1955.

Academy of Psychoanalysis, *Violence and War, with Clinical Studies.* Jules Masserman, ed. Vol. 6 of *Science and Psychoanalysis.* New York: Grune & Stratton, 1963.

Adler, Alfred. "Bolshewismus und Seelenkunde." *International Rundschau,* Zürich, 4 (1918): 15-16.

Adorno, Theodor W. "Zum Verhältnis von Psychoanalyse und Gesellschaftstheorie." *Psyche* 6 (1952): 4-18.

*Adorno, Toeodor W., et al. *The Authoritarian Personality.* New York: Harper Bros., 1950.

Atkin, Samuel. "Notes on Motivation for War: Toward a Psychoanalytic Social Psychology," *Psychoanalytic Quarterly,* 40 (October 1971), 549-83.

Barber, James D. "The Question of Presidential Character," *Saturday Review,* (September 23, 1972): 62-66.

Barbu, Zevedei. *Problems of Historical Psychology.* New York: Grove Press,Inc., 1960.

Barnes, Harry Elmer. "A Psychological Interpretation of Modern Social Problems and of Contemporary History: A Survey of the Contributions of Gustav Le Bon to Social Psychology," *American Journal of Psychology,* 31 (1920): 333-69.

———. *Psychology and History.* New York: Century, 1925.

———. "Psychology and History: Some Reasons for Predicting Their More Active Cooperation in the Future." *American Journal of Psychology* 30 (1920): 300-37.

———. "Some Contributions of American Psychology to Modern Social and Political Theory." *Sociological Review* 13 (1921): 152-167; 204-27.

———. "Some Reflections on the Possible Service of Analytical Psychology to History." *Psychoanalytic Review* 8 (1921): 22-37.

Bartlett, Irving H. and Richard L. Schoenwald, "The Psychodynamics of Slavery," *Journal of Interdisciplinary History,* 4 (Spring 1974), 627-33.

Bartolomei, Giangaetano, "Psicoanalisi et storiografia: Prospettive per un dibattito," *Nuovo Rivista Storica* 56 (1972), 192-203.

Barzun, Jacques. *Clio and the Doctors: Psycho-History, Quanto-History and History.* Chicago: University of Chicago Press, 1974.

———. "History: The Muse and Her Doctors." *American Historical Review* 77 (1972): 36-64. Answering comments by William L. Langer, John J. Fitzpatrick and Peter Loewenberg in "Communications." *American Historical Review* 77 (1972): 1194-197.

Batstein, William. "From the First Part of the Revelation of Moses the Son of Jehoshar" *History of Childhood Quarterly* 1 (1974): 409-36.

Beres, David. "Notes on the History of Morality," *Journal of the American Psychoanalytic Association,* 13 (1965): 3-37.

Bergmann, Martin S. "The Impact of Ego Psychology on the Study of the Myth." *American Imago* 23 (1966).

———. "Limitations of Method in Psychoanalytic Biography: A Historical Inquiry." *Journal of the Psychoanalytic Association* 21 no. 4 (1973): 833.

Berkhofer, Robert F. *A Behavioral Approach to Historical Analysis.* New York: Free Press, 1971.

Bernard, Harold Wright. *Human Development in Western Culture.* Boston: Allyn and Bacon, 1962.

Besdine, M. "Jocasta and Oedipus: Another Look." In *Pathways in Child Guidance.* New York: Bureau of Child Guidance, New York City Board of Education, 1968.

———. "Jocasta Complex, Mothering, and Genius." Part I. *Psychoanalytic Review* 55 (1968): 259-77. Part II. *Psychoanalytic Review* 55 (1968-69): 574-600. Part III. *Psychoanalytic Review* 58 (1971): 51-74.

2

Besançon, Alain. "Psychoanalysis: Auxiliary Science or Historical Method?" *Journal of Contemporary History* 3 (1968): 149-162.

——. "Histoire et Psychoanalyse." *Annales; Economies, Sociétés, Civilisations* 19 (1964): 237-49.

——. "Vers une histoire psychoanalytique." *Annales; Economies, Sociétés, Civilisations* 24 (1969): 594-616 and 1011-33.

Bettelheim, Bruno. "Individual and Mass Behavior in Extreme Situations, *Journal of Abnormal and Social Psychology,* 38 (1943): 417-52.

Birnbach, Martin. *Neo-Freudian Social Philosophy.* London: Oxford University Press, 1962.

Binion, Rudolph, "My Life with *Frau Lou,*" in Perry Curtis, ed., *The Historian's Workshop* (New York, Knopf, 1970), 293-306.

Bonaparte, Marie. "A Defence of Biography," *International Journal of Psycho-Analysis,* 20 (July-October 1939), 231-40.

——. *Myths of War.* London, 1947.

——. "Some Psychoanalytic and Anthropological Insights Applied to Sociology." In *Psychoanalysis and Social Science.* Ed. by Hendrik M. Ruitenbeek. New York: E. P. Dutton & Co., 1962.

Bourde, André. "Un Essai de Psychologie Historique." *Revue Historique* 228 (1962): 35-44.

Bouthoul, Gaston, *Les Guerres: Élements de Polémologie.* Paris, 1951.

*Brown, Norman O. *Life Against Death: The Psychoanalytical Meaning of History.* Middletown, Ct.: Wesleyan Univ. Press, 1959.

——. *Love's Body.* New York: Random House, 1966.

Bushman, Richard L. "On the Use of Psychology: Conflict and Conciliation in Benjamin Franklin." *History and Theory* 5 (1968): 225-40.

Bychowsky, Gustav. "Dictators and Their Followers: A Theory of Dictatorship." *Bulletin Polish Institute of Arts and Sciences in America* 1 (1943): 455-58.

——. "Dictatorship and Paranoia." In *Psychoanalysis and the Social Sciences.* Edited by W. Muensterberger and S. Axelrod. New York: International University Press, 1955, pp. 127-34.

——. *Dictators and Disciples From Caesar to Stalin: A Psychoanalytic Interpretation of History.* New York: International Univ. Press, 1948.

Caenegem, R. van. "Psychologische Geschiedenis." *Tijdschrift von Geschiedenis* 78 (1965): 129-149.

——. "Psychologische geschiedenis," *Spiegel Historial* 4 (1969) 47-53.

Cantril, Hadley. *The Psychology of Social Movements.* NY: Wiley, 1941.

Casey, Robert F. "Oedipus Motivation in Religious Thought and Fantasy." *Psychiatry* 5 (1942): 219-29.

——. "The Psychoanalytic Study of Religion." *Journal of Abnormal and Social Psychology* 33 (1938): 437-52.

Certeau, Michel de, "Ce que Freud Fait de l'histoire, A Propos de 'Une névrose démoniaque ou XVIIᵉ siècle,' " *Annales* 25 (1970): 654-67.

Christie, R. and Marie Jahoda, eds., *Studies in the Scope and Method of "The Authoritarian Personality",* New York: Free Press, 1954.

Claes, Jacques, "Metabletica or a Psychology of History," *Humanitas* 7 (1971) 269-78.

Coles, Robert. *Erik H. Erikson: The Growth of His Work.* Boston: Little, Brown and Co., 1970.

——. "Shrinking History." *New York Review of Books,* 20 (Feb. 22, and March 8, 1973): 15-21; 25-29.

—— and Mazlish, Bruce. "An Exchange on Psychohistory." *New York Review of Books* 26 (May 3, 1973): 36-38.

Combes, André. "La Psychanalyse Freudienne et la Religion Chretienne." *La Table Ronde* 108 (December, 1956): 88.

Dalma, Giovanni. *Psicodinamismo del Matricidio.* Psicoanalisi, Rome: Scienza Moderna, 1948.

Davis, David Brion. "Some Recent Directions in American Cultural History." *American Historical Review* 73 (1968): 696-707.

3

de Becker, Raymond. *The Understanding of Dreams and Their Influence on the History of Men.* New York: Hawthorn Books, 1968.

de Groot, Adrian D. *Saint Nicholas: A Psychoanalytic Study of His History and Myth.* New York: Basic Books, 1965.

Delaunoy, J. "Marxisme et psychanalyse." *Les Feullets Psychiatriques de Liege* 3 (1970): 367-85.

deMause, Lloyd. "The History of Childhood: The Basis for Psychohistory." *History of Childhood Quarterly* 1 (1973): 1-3.

*———. "Psychohistory and Psychotherapy." *History of Childhood Quarterly* 2 (1975): 408-414.

Demos, John. "Demography and Psychology in the Historical Study of Family Life: A Personal Report." In *Household and Family in Past Time.* Edited by Peter Laslett. Cambridge: Cambridge Univ. Press, 1972.

———. "Some Conceptual Problems in the Historical Study of Childhood," paper read at the annual convention of the Organization of American Historians, April 17, 1970, at Los Angeles, Calif.

Dennis, Jack. *Socialization to Politics: A Reader.* New York: John Wiley & Sons, Inc., 1973.

de Rivera, J. H. *The Psychological Dimension of Foreign Policy.* Columbus, Ohio: Charles E. Merrill Publishing Co., 1968.

DeSaussure, Raymond, "Psychoanalysis and History." In *Psychoanalysis and the Social Sciences* 2. Edited by Geza Roheim. New York: International Universities Press, 1950, pp. 7-64.

Devereux, George. "Applied Psychoanalysis: Social Sciences." *The Annual Survey of Psychoanalysis* 2 (1951): 493-538.

———. "Charismatic Leadership and Crisis." In *Psychoanalysis and the Social Sciences.* New York: International Universities Press, 1955, pp. 145-57.

———. *From Anxiety to Method in the Behavioral Sciences.* New York: Humanities Press, 1967.

Dew, Charles B. "Two Approaches to Southern History: Psychology and Quantification," *South Atlantic Quarterly,* 66 (1967): 307-25.

Dicks, Henry V. "The Authoritarian Personality: A Critical Appreciation," *Human Relations,* 4 (1951): 203-11.

DiRenzo, Gordon J., ed. *Personality and Politics.* NY: Doubleday, 1974.

Domhoff, G. William. "Historical Materialism, Cultural Determinism, and the Origin of Ruling Classes," *Psychoanalytic Review,* 56 (1969): 271-87.

Donald, David H. "Between History and Psychology: Reflections on Psychobiography," unpubl. paper delivered at the meeting of the American Psychiatric Association, May 1972.

Doob, Leonard W. "The Analysis and Resolution of International Disputes." *Journal of Psychology* 86 (1974): 313-26.

———. *Patriotism and Nationalism: Their Psychological Foundation.* New Haven: Yale Univ. Press, 1964.

Dooley, Lucille. "Psychoanalytic Studies of Genius," *American Journal of Psychology,* 27 (1916): 363-416.

Dowling, Joseph A. "Psychoanalysis and History: Problems and Applications." *The Psychoanalytic Review* 59 (Fall, 1972): 433-50.

Durbin, E. F. M. and Bowlby, John. *Personal Aggressiveness and War,* New York: Columbia Univ. Press, 1950.

Dunn, Patrick P., "Who Stole the Hyphen from Psycho-History?" *Book Forum* 1 (1974): 248-53.

Easton, David and Dennis, Jack. *Children in the Political System: Origins of Political Legitimacy.* New York: McGraw-Hill Book Co., 1969.

Edel, L. "The Biographer and Psychoanalysis." *International Journal of Psycho-Analysis* 42 (1961): 458-466.

Edinger, Lewis J. "Political Science and Political Biography." *Journal of Politics* 26 (1964): 423-39 and 648-76.

Eiduson, Bernice T. *Scientists: Their Psychological World.* NY: Basic Books, 1962.

Eisenstadt, S. N. *From Generation to Generation: Age Groups and Social Structure.* New York, 1956.

Eissler, Kurt R. "Freud and the Psychoanalysis of History." *Journal of the American Psychoanalytical Association* 11 (Oct., 1963): 605-703.
Erikson, Erik. *Dimensions of a New Identity: The 1973 Jefferson Lectures in the Humanities.* New York: W. W. Norton, 1974.
*———. *Childhood and Society.* New York: W. W. Norton & Co., 1963.
———. "Ego Development and Historical Change." In *The Psychoanalytic Study of the Child.* New York: International Univ. Press, 1946.
———. *Identity and the Life Cycle.* New York: International Univ. Press, 1959.
———. "On the Nature of Psychohistorical Evidence: In Search of Gandhi." In *Philosophers and Kings,* pp. 33-68. Ed. by D. A. Rustow. Also in *Daedalus* 97 (Summer, 1968): 695-730.
———. "Psychoanalysis and Ongoing History: Problems of Identity, Hatred and Nonviolence." *Journal of the American Psychiatric Assn.* 122 (1965): 241-50.
———. "*Verstehen* and the Method of 'Disciplined Subjectivity,' " in Leonard I. Krimerman (ed.), *The Nature and Scope of Social Science: A Critical Anthology.* NY: Appleton-Century-Crofts, 1969, 721-35.

Faber, Michael L. "The Problem of National Character: A Methodological Analysis," *Journal of Psychology,* 30 (1950): 307-316.
Falk, Avner. "Border Symbolism" *The Psychoanalytic Quarterly* 43 (1974): 650-59.
Farber, Maurice L. "Psychoanalytic Hypotheses in the Study of War." *Journal of Social Issues* XI (1955).
Farrell, Brian. "On Freud's Study of Leonardo," in Morris Philipson (ed.), *Leonardo da Vinci: Aspects of the Renaissance Genius* (NY: Braziller, 1966), 224-75.
Fearing, F. "Psychological Studies of Historical Personalities." *Psychological Bulletin* 24 (1927): 520-39.
Feinstein, Howard. "An Application of the Concept of Identification for the Historian," *Journal of the History of the Behavioral Sciences,* 6 (1970): 147-50.
Feldman, A. Bronson. *The Unconscious in History.* NY: Philosophical Library, 1959.
Feuer, Lewis S. *The Scientific Intellectual: Psychological and Sociological Origins of Modern Science.* NY: Basic Books, 1963.
Field, George A. "The Unconscious Organization," *The Psychoanalytic Review* 61 (1974): 333-54.
Fischer, David Hackett. "Fallacies of Motivation." In *Historians' Fallacies Toward a Logic of Historical Thought.* NY: Harper & Row, 1970, 187-215.
Flugel, John C. *The Psychology of Clothes.* London: Hogarth, 1930.
Formisano, Ronald P. "History and the Social Sciences: A Review Essay." *Historical Methods Newsletter* 4 no. 3 (1971): 84-87.
Fornari, Franco, ed. *Dissacrazione della Guerra.* Milan, 1969.
———. *Psicanalisi della Guerra Atomica.* Milan, 1964.
*———. *The Psychoanalysis of War.* NY: Anchor, 1974.
Frank, J. D. *Sanity and Survival: Psychological Aspects of War and Peace.* NY: Random House, 1967.
Freeman, Richard. *Repentance and Revolt: A Psychological Approach to History.* Cranbury, N.J.: Fairleigh Dickinson Univ. Press, 1970.
*Freud, Sigmund. "Civilization and Its Discontents." *Standard Edition* Vol. XXI 64-148.
*———. "The Future of an Illusion." *Standard Edition* Vol. XXI, 5-58.
*———. "Group Psychology and the Analysis of the Ego." *Standard Edition* Vol. XVIII, 69-144.
———. "Thoughts for the Times on War and Death" *Standard Edition* Vol. XIV, 275-302.
———. "Why War?" *Standard Edition* Vol. XXII, 203-15.
*Fromm, Erich. *The Anatomy of Human Destructiveness.* NY: Holt, Rinehart & Winston, 1973.
———. *The Crisis of Psychoanalysis: Essays on Freud, Marx and Social Psychology.* NY: Holt, Rinehart & Winston, 1970.
———. *The Dogma of Christ and Other Essays on Religion.* NY: Holt, Rinehart & Winston, 1963.
*———. *Escape From Freedom.* NY: Farrar & Rinehart, 1941.
———. "Individual and Social Origins of Neurosis." *American Sociological Review*

10 (August, 1944): 380-84. Reprinted in *Personality in Nature, Society and Culture*. Ed. by C. Kluckhohn and H. Murray. NY: Alfred A. Knopf, 1953.
———. "The Limitations and Dangers of Psychology." *Religion and Culture.* Ed. by W. Leibrecht. (Essays in Honor of Paul Tillich.) NY: Harper & Bros, 1959.
———. *Marx's Concept of Man.* NY: Frederick Ungar Publ. Co., 1961.
———. "Die Psychoanalytische Characterologie und Ihre Bedeutung für die Sozialpsychologie." *Zeitschrift für Sozialforschung* 1 (1933): 253-77. Published in English in *The Crisis of Psychoanalysis,* 1970.
———. "Psychoanalyse und Soziologie." *Zeitschrift für Psychoanalytische Pädagogik* 3 (1929): 268-70.
———. *Psychology and Culture.* NY: Holt, Rinehart & Winston, 1963.
———. *The Sane Society.* NY: Rinehart & Co., 1955.
*———. (With Michael Maccoby). *Social Character in a Mexican Village.* Englewood Cliffs, N.J.: Prentice-Hall, 1970.
———. "Theoretische Entwürfe über Autorität und Famillie." *Studien über Autorität und Familie,* pp. 77-135; 230-38. Ed. by Max Horkheimer. Paris: Felix Alcan, 1936.
———. "Zur Psychologie des Verbrechers und der Strafenden Gesellschaft." *Imago* 17 (1931): 226-51.

Garraty, John A. "The Interrelations of Psychology and Biography." *Psychological Bulletin* 51 (November, 1954): 569-82.
———. "Preserved Smith, Ralph Volney Harlow, and Psychology." *Journal of the History of Ideas* 15 (1954): 456-65.
Gedo, John E. "The Methodology of Psychoanalytic Biography." *Journal of the American Psychoanalytic Association* 20 (July, 1972): 638-49.
George, Alexander L. "Power as a Compensatory Value for Political Leaders," *Journal of Social Issues,* 24 (1968): 29-49.
———. "Some Uses of Dynamic Psychology in Political Biography," in Fred I. Greenstein and Michael Lerner, eds., *A Source Book for the Study of Personality and Politics.* Chicago: Markam, 1971.
——— and Juliette L. George, "Psycho-McCarthyism," *Psychology Today,* 7 (June 1973), 94-98.
Goblot, Jean-Jacques. "Histoire et Psychologie." *Pensée* 124 (1965): 86-90
Goldenweiser, A. A. *History, Psychology and Culture.* NY: Knopf, 1933.
Gorer, Geoffrey. "The Concept of National Character." in Kluckhohn, Clyde et al., eds., *Personality in Nature, Society and Culture.* NY, 1948.
Gottschalk, Louis, Kukckhohn, Clyde and Angell, Robert. *The Use of Personal Documents in History, Anthropology and Sociology.* NY: Social Science Research Bulletin, no. 53, 1945.
Graham, Thomas F. *Anatomy of Aggression: Basis of War.* Akron: Beacon-Bell, 1968.
Greenacre, Phyllis, "Treason and the Traitor." *American Imago* 26 (1969): 199-232.
Greenstein, Fred. *Children and Politics.* New Haven: Yale Univ. Press, 1961.
———. *Personality and Politics: Problems of Evidence, Inference and Conceptualization.* Chicago: Markham Publishing Co., 1969.
———. "Private Disorder and the Public Order: A Proposal for Collaboration between Psychoanalysts and Political Scientists," *Psychoanalytic Quarterly,* 37 (1968): 261-81.
——— and Michael Lerner, eds. *A Source Book for the Study of Personality and Politics.* Chicago: Markham Publishing Co., 1971.
Grinspoon, Lester, "Psychological Constraints on the Important Decision Maker," *American Journal of Psychiatry,* 125 (1969): 1074-82.
Group for the Advancement of Psychiatry, "The VIP with Psychiatric Impairment," VIII, Report no. 83, Jan. 1973.
Gruhle, Hans Walter. *Geschichtesschreiben und Psychologie.* Bonn: H. Bonvier, 1953.
Grunberger, Bela. "The Anti-Semite and the Oedipal Conflict." *International Journal of Psycho-Analysis* 45 (1964).
Gurevich, A. Ia. "Nekotorye Aspekty Izerchernia Sotsial'noi Istoril: Obshchestvenno-Istoricheskaia Psikhologia." *Voprosy Istorii* 10 (1964): 51-68.

Haag, Ernest Van Den. "Psychoanalysis and the Social Sciences: Genuine and Spurious Integration." In *Psychoanalysis and Social Science.* Edited by Hendrik M. Ruitenbeek. NY: E. P. Dutton & Co., Inc., 1962.

Hagen, Everett. *On the Theory of Social Change.* Homewood, Ill.: Dorsey Press, 1962.

Hall, Robert. "The Psycho-Philosophy of History," *Main Currents* 29 (1972) 54-61.

Hareven, Tamara K. "The History of the Family as an Interdisciplinary Field." *The Journal of Interdisciplinary History* 2 (1971): 399-414.

Hargrove, Erwin C. *Presidential Leadership: Personality and Political Style.* N.Y.: Macmillan, 1966.

Hartmann, Heinz. "The Application of Psychoanalytic Concepts to Social Science." In *Psychoanalysis and Social Science.* Edited by Hendrik M. Ruitenbeek. NY: E. P. Dutton & Co., Inc., 1962.

Hitschmann, Edward. "Die Bedeutung der Psychoanalyse für die Biographik," *Psychoanalytische Bewegung,* 2 (1930): 305-13.

——. *Great Men: Psychoanalytic Studies.* NY: International Univ. Press, 1956.

——. "Some Aspects of Biography." *International Journal of Psycho-Analysis* 37 (1956): 265-269.

——. "Some Psychoanalytic Aspects of Biography." *International Journal of Psycho-Analysis* 37 (1956): 265-69.

Hoffs, Joshua A. "Comments on Psychoanalytic Biography with Special Reference to Freud's Interest in Woodrow Wilson." *Psychoanalytic Rev.* 56 (1969): 402-14.

Hundert, E. J. "History, Psychology, and the Study of Deviant Behavior." *Journal of Interdisciplinary History* 2 (1972): 453-72.

Inkeles, Alex. "Social Change and Social Character: The Role of Parental Mediation." *Journal of Social Issues* 11 no. 2 (1955): 12-23.

Inkeles, Alex and Levinson, Daniel J. "National Character: The Study of Modal Personality and Sociocultureal Systems." In *Handbook of Social Psychology.* Edited by Gardner Lindsey. Cambridge, Mass.: Addison-Wesley Press, 1954.

Izenberg, Gerald N. "The Logic and Ideology of Psycho-History," paper read at the annual convention of the American Historical Association, Dec. 28, 1971, at New York, N.Y.

*Jaques, Elliott. "Social Systems as a Defence Against Persecutory and Depressive Anxiety" in Melanie Klein, ed., *New Directions in Psycho-Analysis.* NY: Basic Books, 1957.

Jekels, Ludwig. "The Psychology of the Festival of Christmas." *International Journal of Psychiatry* 17 (1936): 57-72.

Jones, Ernest. *Essays in Applied Psychoanalysis.* 2 vol. NY: International Universities Press, Inc., 1964.

——, ed., *Social Aspects of Psychoanalysis.* London: Williams and Norgate, 1924.

Kallen, Horace, "Political Science as Psychology," *American Political Science Rev.,* 17 (1923): 181-203.

Kaplan, M. A. "Psychoanalysis Looks at Politics: A Retrospective Tribute to Robert Waelder." *World Politics* 20 (July, 1968): 699-704.

Kardiner, Abraham. "The Concept of Basic Personality Structure as an Operational Tool in the Social Sciences." In *Personal Character and Cultural Mileu.* Edited by Douglas G. Haring. Syracuse: Syracuse Univ. Press, 1956.

——, ed. *The Individual and His Society.* NY: Columbia Univ. Press, 1939.

——, with the collaboration of Linton, Ralph: Du Bois, Cora; West, James. *The Psychological Frontiers of Society.* NY: Columbia Univ. Press, 1945.

Kelman, Herbert C., ed. *International Behavior: A Social-Psychological Analysis.* NY: Holt, Rinehart and Winston, 1965.

Kelman, Norman. "Social and Psychoanalytical Reflections on the Father." In *Psychoanalysis and Social Science.* Edited by Hendrik M. Ruitenbeek. NY: E. P. Dutton & Co., Inc., 1962.

Keniston, Kenneth. "Accounting for Change." *Comparative Studies in Society and History* 7 (1965): 117-26.

——. "Psychological Development and Historical Change." *Journal of Interdisciplinary History* 2 (1971): 329-45. Reprinted in *The Family in History: Inter-*

disciplinary Essays. 141-58. NY: Harper & Row, 1973.
Kéri, Hedvig. "Ancient Games and Popular Games: Psychological Essay." *American Imago* 15 (1958): 41-89.
Kerr, Madeline. *Personality and Conflict in Jamaica.* Liverpool: Liverpool Univ. Press, 1952.
Kirkinen, Heikki. "Bräiden Psykologian Menetelmien kättämisestä Historiantuki-Muksessa." *Historiallinen Aikakauskirja* 59 no.1 (1961): 37-43.
Kirshner, Lewis A. "Joel Kovel and Robert Jay Lifton: Two Psychohistorical Modes." *The Psychoanalytic Review* 60 (Winter, 1973-74): 613-20.
Kisker, George W., ed. *World Tension: The Psychopathology of International Relations.* NY: Prentice-Hall, 1951.
Klebinder, Ludwig. "Über den Ursprung der Familie." *Zentralblatt für Psychoanalyse und Psychotherapie* 3 (1913): 321-26.
Klineberg, Otto. *The Human Dimension in International Relations.* NY: Holt, Rinehart and Winston, 1964.
———. "A Science of National Character," *Journal of Social Psychology,* 19 (1944): 147-62.
Knutson, Jeanne, ed., *Handbook of Political Psychology.* San Francisco: Jossey-Bass, 1973.
Kovel, Joel. "Erik Erickson's Psychohistory." *Social Policy* (1974). 60-64.
Kren, George M. and Rappoport, Leon. "Clio and Psyche." *History of Childhood Quarterly* 1 (1973): 151-63.
———. "Psychohistory: Methodology as Ideology." Unpublished paper delivered at CHERION annual meeting, May 31, 1974.
Kroner, Bernhard, "Psychologie und Präsentismus," *Das Argument* no. 75 (1972): 56-75.
Kunstmann, Josef. *The Transformation of Eros.* Edinburgh, 1964.
Kurth, Gertrude M. "Politics: Unconscious Factors in Social Prejudice and Mass Movements." In *Elements of Psychoanalysis,* ed. by Kurth, Gertrude M. and Herman, Hans. Cleveland, Ohio: World Publishing Co., 1950, pp. 297-309.

La Barre, Weston. *The Ghost Dance: Origins of Religion.* Garden City: Doubleday & Co., 1970.
Lane, Robert E., "Personality, Political: The Study of Political Personality," in D. Shils, ed., *International Encyclopedia of the Social Sciences.* NY: Macmillan, 1968.
———. "Political Science and Psychology." In *Psychology: A Study of a Science,* Vol. 6, 583-638. Ed. by S. Koch. NY: McGraw-Hill, 1963.
Langer, W. L. "Next Assignment." *American Historical Review* 68 (1958): 283-304. Reprinted in *Psychoanalysis and History,* ed. by Bruce Mazlish. NY: Grosset and Dunlap, 1971, 87-107.
Lasswell, Harold D. *The Analysis of Political Behavior.* London: Kegan Paul, 1947.
———. "Approach to Human Personality: William James and Sigmund Freud." *Psychoanalysis and the Psychoanalytic Review* 47 (1960): 52-68.
———. "The Contribution of Freud's Insight Interview to the Social Sciences." *American Journal of Sociology* 45 (1939): 375-90.
———. "Impact of Psychoanalytic Thinking on the Social Sciences." In *State of the Social Sciences,* pp. 84-115. Ed. by L. D. White. Reprinted in *Psychoanalysis and Social Science.* Ed. by Hendrik M. Ruitenbeek. NY: E. P. Dutton & Co., Inc., 1962.
———. "Political Constitution and Character." *Psychoanalysis and the Psychoanalytic Review* 46 (1959): 3-18.
———. *Power and Personality.* NY: Viking, 1948.
———. "Propaganda and Mass Insecurity." *The Psychoanalytic Review* 41 (1954): 78.
*———. *Psychopathology and Politics.* New edition with afterthoughts by author. NY: Viking Press, 1960.
———. *World Politics and Personal Insecurity.* NY: McGraw-Hill, 1935.
———. "What Psychiatrists and Political Scientists Can Learn from One Another." *Psychiatry* I (1938): 33-39.
——— and Blumenstock, D. "The Technique of Slogans in Communist Propaganda." *Psychiatry* 1 (1938): 505-20.

Lederer, Wolfgang, "Historical Consequences of The Father-Son Hostility," *Psychoanalytic Review,* 54 (1967): 52-80.

Lehner, Fritz, "Zum Thema Biographik und Psychoanalyse," *Psychoanalytische Bewegung,* 5 (1933): 201-02.

Leites, Nathan, "Psycho-Cultural Hypotheses about Political Acts," *World Politics,* 1 (1948): 102-19.

Levin, A. J. "The Oedipus Myth in History and Psychiatry: A New Interpretation." *Psychiatry* 11 (1948): 283-99.

LeVine, Robert A. *Culture, Behavior, and Personality.* Chicago: Aldine, 1973.

Lévy-Valensi, E. A. "Histoire et Psychologie?" *Annales* 20 (1965): 923-38.

Lewin, Rom. "Psychoanalysis and Social Change." *Psychoanalytic Review* 54 (1967): 66-76.

Lifton, Robert Jay. "Comments on Method." *Contemporary Studies in Society and History* 7 (1965): 127-32.

————. *History and Human Survival; Essays on the Young and Old, Survivors and the Dead, Peace and War, and on Contemporary Psychohistory.* NY: Random House, 1970.

————. "On Death and the Continuity of Life: A 'New' Paradigm" *History of Childhood Quarterly,* 1 (1974): 681-96.

————. "On Psychohistory." In *The State of American History.* Ed. by Herbert J. Bass. Chicago: Quadrangle, 1970: 276-92.

————. "Psychohistory." *Partisan Review* 37 no. 1 (1970): 11-32.

————. "Protean Man." In *Psychoanalytic Interpretation of History.* Ed. by B. R. Wolman. NY: Basic Books, 1971.

————, ed. *Explorations in Psychohistory.* New York: Simon and Schuster, 1975.

Lipshire, Sidney. "Herbert Marcuse and the Search for a Revolutionary Dialectic: From Marx to Freud and Beyond," paper read at the annual convention of the American Historical Association, December 28, 1972, at New Orleans, La.

Little, Lester K. "Psychology in Recent American Historical Thought." *Journal of the History of the Behavioral Sciences* 5 (1969): 152-72.

London, Ivan D. and Poltoratzky, Nikolai P. "The Problem of Contemporary Analysis in History and Psychology." *Behavioral Sciences* 3 (1958): 269-77.

Lorenz, Emil Franz. *Der Politische Mythers. Beiträge zur Mythologie der Kultur.* n.p.: Internationaler Psychoanalytischer Verlag, 1923, 1925, 1931.

————. *Zur Psychologie der Politik.* Klagenfurt: Heyn, 1919.

Lowenfeld, Henry. "Freud's *Moses* and Bismarck." In *The Psychoanalytic Study of the Child,* ed. by Ruth S. Eissler, Anna Freud, Heinz Hartmann, and Ernst Kris. NY: International Univ. Press, 1950: 277-90.

Lowtzky, Fanny. "Mahatma Gandhi: A Contribution to the Psychoanalytic Understanding of the Causes of Wars, and the Means of Preventing Them." *International Journal of Psycho-Analysis* 33 no. 4 (1952): 485-88.

McClelland, David C. "Why and How to Code the Psychological Content of Historical Documents," paper read at the annual convention of the Organization of American Historians, April 8, 1972, at Washington, D.C.

Mack, John E. "Psychoanalysis and Historical Biography." *Journal of American Psychoanalytical Association* 19 (1971): 143-79.

Madden, Edward H. "Explanation in Psychoanalysis and History," *Philosophy of Science,* 33 (1966): 278-86.

Mandelbaum, D. G. "Study of Life History: Gandhi." *Current Anthropology* 14 (1973): 177-206.

Mandle, W. F. "Psychology and History." *New Zealand Journal of History* 2, no. 1 (1968): 1-17.

Manuel, Frank E. "Use and Abuse of Psychology in History." *Daedalus* 100 (1971): 187-213. Reprinted in *Historical Studies Today,* ed. by Felix Gilbert and Stephen R. Graubard. NY: Norton, 1972: 211-37.

————. "Toward a Psychological History of Utopia." *Daedalus* 94 (1965): 293-322.

*Marcuse, Herbert. *Eros and Civilization: A Philosophical Inquiry Into Freud.* Boston: The Beacon Press, 1955.

————. *Psychoanalyse u. Politik.* Frankfurt, 1968.

————. "The Social Implications of Freudian Revisionism," *Dissent,* 2 (1955): 221-40.

Matson, F. W. "History as Act: The Psychological-Romantic View." *Journal of History of Ideas* 18 (1957): 270-79.

May, Rollo. *Power and Innocence: A Search for the Sources of Violence.* NY: Norton, 1972.

Mazlish, Bruce. "Autobiography and Psycho-Analysis." *Encounter* 33 (1970).

———. "Clio on the Couch. Prolegomenia to Psycho-History." *Encounter* 31 (1968): 46-54.

———. "Group Psychology and Problems of Contemporary History." *Journal of Contemporary History* 3 no. 2 (1968).

———. "History and Psychiatry." In *American Handbook of Psychiatry.* Vol. I. Ed. by Silvana Arieti. NY: Basic Books, 1974: 1034-45.

———. "Inside the Whales." *The Times Literary Supplement* 3361 (July 28, 1966): 667-69.

*———, ed. *Psychoanalysis and History.* Englewood Cliffs, N.J.: Prentice-Hall, 1963. Rev. ed., NY: Grosset & Dunlap, 1971.

———. Review Essay. *The Iron Cage: An Historical Interpretation of Max Weber.* By Arthur Mitzman. NY: Alfred A. Knopf, 1969. *History and Theory* X no. 1 (1970): 90-107.

———. "Towards a Psycho-Historical Inquiry: The 'Real' Richard Nixon." *Journal of Interdisciplinary History* 1 (1970): 49-105.

———. "What is Psycho-History?" *Treatises of the Royal History Society* [Great Britain] 21 (1971): 79-99.

Merriam, Charles E. "The Significance of Psychology for the Study of Politics." *American Political Science Review,* 18 (1924): 469-488.

Meyer, Bernard C. "Some Reflections on the Contribution of Psychoanalysis to Biography." In *Psychoanalysis and Contemporary Science,* pp. 373-92. Ed. by Robert R. Holt and Emanuel Peterfreund. NY: The Macmillan Co., 1972.

Meyer, Donald B. "A Review of *Young Man Luther: A Study in Psychoanalysis and History.*" *History and Theory* 1 (1961): 291-97.

Meyerhoff, Hans. "Freud and the Ambiguity of Culture," in Bruce Mazlish, ed., *Psychoanalysis and History.* NY: Grosset & Dunlap, 1971: 56-68.

———. "On Psychoanalysis and History." *Psychoanalysis and the Psychoanalytical Review* 49 no. 2 (1962): 3-20.

Mintz, Ira L. "Unconscious Motives in the Making of War." *Medical Opinion and Review* (1968): 88-95.

Money-Kyrle, Roger E. "The Development of War." *British Journal of Medical Psychology* 16 (1937).

———. *The Meaning of Sacrifice.* London: Hogarth Press, 1929. Reprinted with the permission of the Hogarth Press Ltd. NY: Johnson Reprint Corp., 1929.

*———. *Psychoanalysis and Politics.* New York: W. W. Norton & Co., Inc., 1951. Englewood Cliffs: Prentice Hall, 1963.

———. "Some Aspects of Political Ethics from the Psychoanalytic Point of View," *International Journal of Psycho-Analysis,* 25 (1944): 166-71.

Morse, Nancy Carter & Allport, F. H. "The Causation of Anti-Semitism; an Investigation of Seven Hypotheses." *Journal of Psychology* 34 (1952): 197-233.

Murphy, H. B. M. "Social Change and Mental Health." *Millbank Memorial Fund Quarterly* 39 (1961): 385-445.

Nadel, George. "History as Psychology in Francis Bacon's Theory of History." *History and Theory* 5 no. 3 (1966): 275-87.

Nelson, Banjamin, ed. *Freud and the Twentieth Century.* Gloucester, Mass.: Peter Smith, 1958.

———. "Psychoanalysis and Psychohistory—An Analytic Perspective." *Book Forum* 1 (1974): 254-62.

Nissenbaum, Stephen. "Sex, Reform and Social Change," paper read at the annual convention of the Organization of American Historians, April 7, 1972, at Washington, D.C.

Norwood, William Frederick. "Psychopathology and History." *Medical Arts and Sciences: Journal of Loma Linda University School of Medicine,* 22 (1968): 63-66.

Obuchowski, Kazimierz, "Zastosowanie hipotez psychologicznych w naukach historycznych. *Studia Metodologiczne* 9 (1972): 57-78.
Opler, Marvin K., Ed. *Culture and Mental Health.* NY: The Macmillan Co., 1959.
Orlow, Dietrich. "The Significance of Time and Place in Psychohistory." *The Journal of Interdisciplinary History* 5 (1974): 131-38.
Ostwald, Wilhelm. *Grosse Männer.* Leipzig: Akademische Verlagsgesellschaft, 1910.

Parsons, Talcott, "Psychoanalysis and the Social Structure." In *Psychoanalysis and Social Science.* Ed. by Hendrik M. Ruitenbeek. NY: E. P. Dutton & Co., Inc., 1962.
——. *Social Structure and Personality.* NY: The Free Press, 1964, 1970.
Patterson, James T. "The Uses of Techno-Psychohistory." *The Journal of Interdisciplinary History* 2 no. 4 (1972): 473-76.
Pear. T. H., ed. *Psychological Factors of Peace and War.* NY: Philosophical Library, Inc., 1951.
Peeters, H. F. M. "Prolegomenia van een psychologische Geschiedenis." *Tijdschrift voor Geschiedenis* 80 no. 1 (1967): 23-38.
Pye, Lucian W. "Personal Identity and Political Ideology," in Bruce Mazlish, ed., *Psychoanalysis and History.* NY: Grosset & Dunlap, 1971: 150-73.
Pomper, Philip. "Problems of a Naturalistic Psychohistory." *History and Theory* 12 (December, 1973): 367-88.

Rank, Otto. *Das Inzestmotif in Dichtung und Saga.* Vienna: F. Deuticke, 1912. Translated in Philip Freund, ed. *Myth of the Birth of the Hero.* NY: Random House, 1959.
Ratner, Sidney. "The Historian's Approach to Psychology." *Journal of the History of Ideas* 2 (1941): 95-109.
Renshon, Stanley Allen. *Psychological Needs and Political Behavior: A Theory of Personality and Political Efficacy.* NY: Free Press, 1974.
Reiff, Philip. "The Authority of the Past." In *The Mind of the Moralist.* NY: The Viking Press, Inc., 1959.
——. "The Authority of the Past—Sickness and Society in Freud's Thought." *Social Research* (Winter, 1954).
——. "The Meaning of History and Religion in Freud's Thought," in Bruce Mazlish, ed., *Psychoanalysiʳ and History.* NY: Grosset and Dunlap, 1971: 23-44.
——. "History, Psychoanalysis and the Soʲial Sciences." *Ethics* (Jan., 1953).
——. "Psychology and Politics: The Freudian Connection." *World Politics* 7 no. 2 (1955): 293-305.
——. "Toward a Theory of Culture: With Special Reference to the Psychoanalytic Case." In *Imagination and Precision in the Social Sciences,* pp. 97-98. Ed. by T. J. Nossiter et al. London, 1972.
——. "The Triumph of the Therapeutic." In *The Triumph of the Therapeutic,* pp. 238-61. NY: Harper & Row, 1966.
Reik, Theodor. "Zum Gottesglauben des Kindes." *Zeitschrift für Psychoanalytische Pädagogik* 2 (1927-28): 61.
Riegel, K. F. "History as a nomethetic Science: Some Generalizations From Theories and Research in Developmental Psychology." *The Journal of Social Issues* 25 (Autumn, 1969): 99-127;
Roazen, Paul. *Freud: Political and Social Thought.* NY: Knopf, 1968.
Rogow, Arnold. "Disability in High Office," *Medical Opinion and Review,* 1 (1966): 16-19.
——. "Psychiatry, History and Political Science: Notes on an Emergent Synthesis. " In *Modern Psychoanalysis: New Directions and Perspectives.* Ed. by Judd Marmor. NY: Basic Books, 1968.
——. "Psychiatry as a Political Science," *Psychiatric Quarterly,* 40 (1966): 319-32.
——. "Some Psychiatric Aspects of Political Science and Political Life." In *Social Psychology and Political Behavior: Problems and Prospectives.* Ed. by Gilbert Abcarian and J. W. Soule. Columbus: Charles E. Merrill, 1971.
——. "Toward a Psychiatry of Politics." In *Politics, Personality and Social Science in the Twentieth Century: Essays in Honor of Harold D. Lasswell,* pp. 123-45. Ed. by Arnold A. Rogow. Chicago: University of Chicago Press, 1969.

Roheim, Geza. "The Evolution of Culture." In *Psychoanalysis and History*. Ed. by Bruce Mazlish. Englewood Cliffs, N.J.: Prentice-Hall, Inc., 1963.
*———. *The Origin and Function of Culture*. Nervous and Mental Disease Monographs No. 69. NY, 1943.
———. "Psychoanalysis and Anthropology." In *Psychoanalysis and Social Science*. Ed. by Hendrik M. Ruitenbeek. NY: E. P. Dutton & Co., Inc., 1962.
———. "The Psycho-Analytic Interpretation of Culture." *International Journal of Psycho-Analysis* 22 (1941): 147-69.
———. "The Study of Character Development and the Ontogenetic Theory of Culture." In *Essays Presented to C. G. Seligman*, pp. 28-293. London: Kegan Paul, 1933.
———. "War, Crime and the Covenant." *Journal of Crim. Psychopath.* 4 (1943): 731-45. *Journal of Crim. Psychopath.* 5 (1944): 143-65; 363-405; 597-626.
Rolle, Andrew. "Biological Aggression and Human Irrationality," paper read at the annual convention of the American Historical Association, Dec. 28, 1971, at New York, N.Y.
Roszak, Theodore. "The Historian as Psychiatrist," *The Nation*, 195 (Nov. 24, 1962): 343-48.
Rutherford, B. "Psychopathology, Decision-Making and Political Involvement," *Journal of Conflict Resolution*, 10 (1966): 387-407.

*Saffady, William. "Manuscripts and Psychohistory," *American Archivist*, 37 (1974): 551-64.
Schaffner, Bertram. Discussion of Lasswell, H. D. "Psychoanalytic Conceptions in Political Science." In *Science and Psychoanalysis*, pp. 76-77. Ed. by J. H. Masserman. NY: Greene and Stratton, 1961.
Schaar, John H. *Escape From Authority: The Perspectives of Erich Fromm.* NY: Basic Books, 1961.
Schlesinger, Arthur, Jr. "Can Psychiatry Save the Republic?" *Saturday Review/World*, Sept. 7, 1974, pp. 10-16.
Schmidl, Fritz. "Psychoanalysis and History." *Psychoanalytic Quarterly* 31 (Oct. 1962): 539-43.
———. "Problems of Method in Applied Psychoanalysis." *The Psychoanalytic Quarterly* 41 (1972): 402-19.
Schoenwald, Richard L. "Historians and the Challenge of Freud." *Western Humanities Review* 10 (1956): 99-108.
———. "Sigmund Freud: The Origins and Early Development of a Social Theory," unpublished doctoral dissertation, Harvard Univ., 1952.
———. "Using Psychology in History: A Review Essay." *Historical Methods Newsletter* 7 (1973): 9-24.
Seeley, John R. "The Americanization of the Unconscious." In *Psychoanalysis and Social Science*. Ed. by Hendrik M. Ruitenbeek. NY: E. P. Dutton & Co., Inc., 1962, pp. 186-99.
———. "Psychoanalysis: A Model for Social Science." In *Psychoanalysis and Social Science*. Ed. by Hendrik M. Ruitenbeek. NY: E. P. Dutton & Co., Inc., 1962, pp. 102-11.
*Simmel, Ernst, ed. *Anti-Semitism: A Social Disease.* Preface by Gordon W. Allport. NY: International Univ. Press, 1946.
Singer, J. David. "Man and World Politics: The Psycho-Cultural Interface," *Journal of Social Issues*, 24 (1968): 127-56.
Smith, Page. "Anxiety and Despair in American History." *William and Mary Quarterly* s3 26 (July, 1969): 416-24.
Snyder, Milton. "A Survey of Culture and Personality Theory and Research." In *Studying Personality Cross-Culturally*. Ed. by Bert Kaplan. Evanston, 1961.
Spitzer, Alan P. "The Historical Problem of Generations." *American Historical Review* 78 (December, 1973): 1353-85.
Stark, S., "Toward a Psychology of Charisma: I. The Innovative Viewpoint of Robert Tucker," *Psychological Reports*, 23 (1968): 1163-66; "Toward a Psychology of Charisma: II. The Pathology Viewpoint of James C. Davis," *Psychological Reports*, 24 (1969): 88-90.
Strachey, Alix. *The Unconscious Motives of War: A Psycho-Analytical Contribution.* NY: International Universities Press, Inc., 1957.

———. "Psychological Problems of Nationhood." *The Year Book of World Affairs* (1960): 260-85.

Strickland, D. A. "Non-Vivus Psychoanalysis of Political Figures: A Review." *Journal of Conflict Resolution* 11 (1967): 375-81.

Strout, Cushing. "Ego Psychology and the Historian." *History and Theory* 7 no. 3 (1968): 281-97.

*Taylor, G. Rattray. *Sex in History*. London: Thames and Hudson, rev. ed. 1959.

TeSelle, Sallie, ed. *The Family, Communes, and Utopian Societies*. New York, 1971.

Torres, Mauro. "La Psicologia en La Historia." *Boletin Cultural y Bibliografico* [Colombia] 13 (1970): 5-15.

Toynbee, Arnold J. "Aspects of Psycho-History," *Main Currents* 29 (1972): 44-46.

Treher, Wolfgang. *Hegels Geisteskrankheit, oder das verborgene Gesicht der Geschichte; psychopathologische Untersuchungen und Betrachtungen über das historische Prophetentum*. Emmendingen: W. Treher 1969.

Trilling, Lionel. *Freud and the Crisis of our Culture*. Boston: The Beacon Press, 1955.

Tuchman, Barbara W. "Can History Use Freud?" *Atlantic Monthly* 219 (1967): 39-45.

Waelder, R. "Psychoanalysis and History: Application of Psychoanalysis to Historiography." In *Psychoanalytic Interpretation of History*. Ed. by B. R. Wohlman. NY: Basic Books, 1971.

Walker, Patrick Chrestien Gordon. "History and Psychology." *Social Review* 37 (1947): 37 49.

Walsh, M. N., "Psychoanalytic Studies of War." *Philadelphia Assoc. of Psychoanalysis Bulletin* 12 (1962).

Walsh, W. H. "Review Essay of Robert Berkhofer's *A Behavioral Approach to Historical Analysis* (NY: The Free Press, 1969). *History and Theory* 10 no. 2 (1971): 241-46.

*Wangh, Martin. "A Psychogenetic Factor in the Recurrence of War." *International Journal of Psycho-Analysis* 49 (1968): 319-23.

Watson, Goodwin. "Clio and Psyche: Some Interrelations of Psychology and History." In *The Cultural Approach to History*. Ed. by Caroline F. Ware. NY: Columbia Univ. Press, 1940.

Wehler, Hans-Ulrich. *Geschichte und Psychanalyse*. Cologne, 1971.

———. "Zum Verhältnis von Geschichtswissenschaft und Psychoanalyse." *Historische Zeitschrift* 208 (1969): 529-54.

Weinstein, Fred and Gerald Platt. "Alienation and the Problem of Social Action," in Edward A. Tiryakian, ed., *The Phenomenon of Sociology*. NY: Appleton-Century-Crofts, 1971: 284-310.

———. "The Coming Crisis in Psychohistory," forthcoming in *Journal of Modern History*, June 1975.

———. "History and Theory: The Question of Psychoanalysis." *Journal of Interdisciplinary History* 2 (1972): 419-34.

———. *Psychoanalytic Sociology: An Essay on the Interpretations of Historical Data and the Phenomenon of Collective Behavior*. Baltimore: Johns Hopkins Univ. Press, 1973.

*Weisskopf, Walter A. *The Psychology of Economics*. Chiacgo, 1955.

Wilbur, George B. and Muensterberg, Warner, eds. *Psychoanalysis and Culture: Essays in Honor of Geza Roheim*. NY: International Univ. Press, 1965.

Willcox, William B. "The Psychiatrist, the Historian and General Clinton: The Excitement of Historical Research." *Michigan Quarterly Review* 6 (1961): 123-30.

Winnik, Heinrich Z. "Psychoanalytical Thought on the Concept of National Character," *The Israel Annals of Psychiatry*, 11 (1973): 173-88.

———, et al., eds. *Psychological Basis of War*. NY: Quadrangle, 1973.

Wittkower, Rudolf and M. Wittkower. *Born Under Saturn: The Character and Conduct of Artists: A Documented History from Antiquity to the French Revolution*. NY: Random House, 1963.

Wolfenstein, E. Victor. *Personality and Politics*. Belmont, Calif.: Dickenson, 1969.

———. "Some Psychological Aspects of Crisis Leaders," in Lewis Edinger, ed., *Political Leadership in Industrialized Societies*. NY: John Wiley & Sons, 1967: 155-81.

Wolman, Benjamin. "Evidence in Psychoanalytic Research." *Journal of the American Psychoanalytic Association* 12 (1964): 717-33.
——, ed. *The Psychoanalytic Interpretation of History.* NY: Basic Books, 1971.
——. "Sense and Nonsense in History," in Benjamin B. Wolman, ed., *The Psychoanalytic Interpretation of History.* NY: Basic Books, 1971: 79-114.
Wyatt, Frederick. "In Quest of Change: Comments on Robert J. Lifton's Individual Patterns and Historical Change." *Comparative Studies in Society and History* 6 (1964): 384-92.
——. "Psychoanalytic Biography," *Contemporary Psychology,* 1 (1964): 105-07.
——. "A Psychologist Looks at History." *Journ. of Soc. Issues* 16 (1961): 182-90.
——. "The Reconstruction of the Individual and of the Collective Past." In *The Study of Lives,* ed. by Robert W. White. NY: Prentice-Hall, 1963: 304-20.

Zaleznik, Abraham. "Charismatic and Consensus Leaders: A Psychological Comparison," *Bulletin of the Menninger Clinic,* 38 (1974): 222-38.

II. THE HISTORY OF CHILDHOOD

Abbott, Edith. "A Study of the Early History of Child Labor in America." *The American Journal of Sociology* XIV (1908): 15-37.
Abbott, Grace. *The Child and the State.* 2 Vols. Chicago: The University of Chicago Press, 1938.
Aland, Kurt. *Did the Early Church Baptize Infants?* London, 1962.
Alberti, Leo B. *The Family in Renaissance Florence.* Columbia: Univ. of S. Carolina Press, 1969.
Alpert, Augusta. "Reactions to the Assassination of the President." *The Psychoanalytic Study of the Child* 19 (1964).
Anderson, John. "Child Development: An Historical Perspective." *Child Development* 27 (1956): 181-96.
Anshen, R. *The Family, Its Function and Destiny.* Science of Culture Series, Vol. 5. NY: Harper, 1949.
Antoniadis-Bibicou, H. "Quelques notes sur l'enfant de la moyenne epoque byzantine (VIᵉ-XII siecles). *Annales de Demographie Historique* (1973): 77-84.
*Ariès, Philippe. *Centuries of Childhood.* NY: Alfred A. Knopf, 1962.
Armengaud, A. "L'Attitude de la societe a l'egard de l'enfant au XIX siecle." *Annals de Demographie Historique* (1973): 303-10.
Arnold, Cari. *Das Kind in der deutschen Literatur des XI-XV Jahrhunderts.* Griefswald, 1905.
Atkins, Norman B. "The Oediups Myth, Adolescence, and the Succession of Generations." *Journal of the American Psychoan. Assoc.* 18 (1970).
Avery, Gillian. *Nineteenth Century Children: Heroes and Heroines in English Children's Stories, 1780-1900.* London, 1965.

Bach, George R. "Father-Fantasies and Father-Typing in Father-Separated Children." *Child Development* 17 (1946): 63-80.
*Bakan, David. *Slaughter of the Innocents: A Study of the Battered Child Phenomenon.* San Francisco: Jossey-Bass, 1971.
Batany, J. "Regards sur l'enfance dans la literature moralisante." *Annales de Demographie Historique* (1973): 123-28.
Bayne-Powell, Rosamond. *The English Child in the Eighteenth Century.* London: Murray, 1939.
Beck, A. G. *Greek Education: 450-350 B.C.* London, 1964.
Bedford, Jessie (pseud. Elizabeth Godfrey). *English Children in the Olden Time.* London: Methuen & Co., 1907.
Benedict, Ruth. "Child Rearing in Certain European Countries." *American Journal of Orthopsychiatry* 19 (1949): 345-46.
Benjamin, Nancy. *Children in Need.* Cincinnati: Friendship Press, 1966.
Bennett, H. "Exposure of Infants in Ancient Rome." *Classical Journal* 18 (1923): 341-45.
Berkner, Lutz K. "Recent Research on the History of the Family in Western Eu-

rope," *Journal of Marriage and the Family* 35 (1973): 395-405.
Besdine, Matthew. "Jewish Mothering." *Jewish Spectator* 35 (1970): 7-10.
Bett, Henry. *The Games of Children: Origin and History.* London, 1929.
Bettelheim, Bruno. *Children of the Dream.* NY, 1969.
Biraben, J. N. "La medicine et l'enfant au Moyen Age." *Annales de Demographie Historique* (1973): 73-76.
———. "Le medicin et l'enfant au XVIII siecle." *Annales de Demographie Historique* (1973): 215-24.
Bissel, Linda Auwers, "From One Generation to Another: Mobility in Seventeenth-Century Windsor, Connecticut." *The William and Mary Quarterly,* 3d ser., 31 (1974): 79-110.
Blummer, H. *The Home Life of the Ancient Greeks.* NY: Cooper Square, 1966.
Boas, George. *The Cult of Childhood.* London, 1966.
Bolkestein, H. "The Exposure of Children at Athens." *Classical Phil.* 17, 1922.
Bonde, Amédé. *Etude sur L'infanticide, L'exposition et la conditiondes enfants exposés en droit romain.* Paris, 1883.
Bossard, James and Boll, Eleanor. *Sociology of Child Development.* 3rd ed. NY, 1960.
Braun, Samuel J. and Esther P. Edwards. *History and Theory of Early Childhood Education.* Worthington, Ohio: Charles A. Jones Publishing, 1972.
*Bremner, Robert. *Childhood and Youth in America: A Documentary History.* 3 vols. Cambridge, Mass.: Harvard Univ. Press, 1970-74.
Brenner, Joseph H. and Coles, Robert. *Children of Crisis.* Boston, 1967.
Brissaud, Y. B. "L'Infanticide a la fin du moyen age, ses motivations psychologiques et sa repression." *Revue Historique de Droit Francais et etranger* 50 (1972): 229-56.
Bronardel, P. *L'Infanticide.* Paris, 1897.
Bronfenbrenner, Urie. "The Changing American Child: A Speculative Analysis." *Journal of Social Issues* 17 (1961): 6-18.
———. "Socialization and Social Class Through Time and Space." In *Readings in Social Psychology.* Ed. by E. C. Moscoby, et al. NY, 1958.
———. *Two Worlds of Childhood: US and USSR.* NY, 1970.
Bronson, Wanda S.; Katten, Edith S.; Livson, Norman. "Patterns of Authority and Affection in Two Generations." *Journal of Abnormal and Social Psychology* 58 (1959): 143-52.
Brown, Ann Duncan, comp. *Youth Movement in the United States and Foreign Countries.* Washington, D.C., 1936.
Burgess, Ernest W., Locke, Harvey J., Thomes, Mary Margaret. *The Family: From Tradition to Companionship.* NY: Van Nostrand, 1971.
Burlingham, Dorothy T. "Precursors of Some Psychoanalytic Ideas About Children in the Sixteenth and Seventeenth Centuries." In *The Annual Survey of Psychoanalysis,* pp. 17-19. Ed. by John Frosch. NY, 1954.

Calhoun, Arthur W. *A Social History of the American Family From Colonial Times to the Present.* 3 vols. NY, 1945.
Calvet, J. *Le'enfant dans la literature francaise.* Paris, 1930. Reprint of 1870 edition.
Cameron A. "The Exposure of Children and Greek Ethics." *Classical Review* 46 (1932): 105-14.
Carsch, H. "The Family, Child-Rearing and Social Controls Among the Aztecs." *International Anthropological and Linguistic Review* 3, 1958.
Caudill, William and Weinstein, Helen. "Maternal Care and Infant Behavior in Japan and America." *Psychiatry* 32, 1969.
Caulfield, Ernest. *The Infant Welfare Movement in the Eighteenth Century.* NY: Paul B. Hoeber, 1931.
———. "Some Common Diseases of Colonial Children." *Publications of the Colonial Society of Massachusetts* XXXV, 1942-46.
Chadwick, Mary. *Adolescent Girlhood.* NY: John Day, 1933.
———. "Die Gott-Phantasie bei Kinderns." *Imago* 13 (1927): 383-94.
———. "Kinderheitserlebnisse von Pflegerinnen kleiner Kinder." *Zeitschrift für Psychoanalytische Pädagogik* 7 (1933): 322-33.
Chamberlain, Alexander F. *Child and Childhood in Folk Thought.* Reprint of

1896 edition. Ann Arbor, Mich.: The Finch Press, n.d.

Chamoux, A. "L'enfance abondonnee a Reims a la fine du XVIIIe siecle." *Annales de Demographie Historique* (1973): 263-86.

Chapman, Arthur H. "Obsessions of Infanticide." *Archive of Gen. Psych.* 1 (1959): 12-16.

Charpentier, Jehanne. *Le Droit de l'enfance Abandonee.* Paris, 1967.

Chateauneuf, Louis Benoiston de. *Considerations sur les enfants trouves dans les principaux etats de l'Europe.* Paris, 1824.

Chrisman, Oscar. *The Historical Child.* Boston: Badger, 1920.

Comfort, Alex. *The Anxiety Makers.* Los Angeles: Dell Publ. Co., Inc., 1970.

Corvisier, A. "La societe militaire et l'enfant." *Annales de Demographie Historique* (1973): 327-44.

Coulton, G. G. *Infant Perdition in the Middle Ages.* London: Simpkin, 1922.

Cournot, L. *La repression de l'infanticide.* Angers, 1885.

Coveney, Peter. *The Image of Childhood: The Individual and Society: A Study of the Theme in English Literature.* Baltimore, 1967.

Craig, William Ellwood. "Vincent of Beauvais On the Education of Noble Children." University of Calif., Los Angeles, Ph.D. thesis, 1949.

Crandall, John C. "Patriotism and Humanitarian Reform in Children's Literature, 1825-1860." *American Quarterly* 2 (1969): 3-22.

Cremin, Lawrence A. *American Education: The Colonial Experience 1607-1783.* NY: Harper & Row, 1970.

————. "The Family as Educator: Some Comments on the Recent Historiography." *Teachers College Record* 76 (1974): 250-65.

Crump, Lucy. *Nursery Life Three Hundred Years Ago: The Story of a Dauphin of France, 1601-10.* London: George Routledge, 1929.

Cunningham, Phillis and Buck, Anne. *Children's Costume in England. Thirteen Hundred to Nineteen Hundred.* Scranton, Pa.: Barnes & Noble, 1965.

Darlington, H. S. "Ceremonial Behaviorism: Sacrifices For the Foundation of Houses." *The Psychoanalytic Review* 18, 1931.

Davis, Allison and Dollard, John. *Children of Bondage: The Personality Development of Negro Youth in the Urban South.* Scranton, Pa., n.d.

Davis, Allison and Havighurst, Robert J. "Social Class and Color Differences in Child-Rearing." *American Sociological Review* 11 (1943): 698-710.

Davis, Natalie Z. "The Reasons of Misrule: Youth Groups and Charivaris in Sixteenth-Century France." *Past and Present* L (1971): 41-75.

DeHaussy J. *L'Assistance publique à l'enfance. Les enfants abandonnés.* Paris, 1951.

Delzons, L. *La famille française et son évolution.* Paris, 1913.

*deMause, Lloyd. "The Evolution of Childhood." In *The History of Childhood.* Ed. by Lloyd deMause. NY: The Psychohistory Press, 1974. Also as symposium in *History of Childhood Quarterly* 1 (1974): 503-606.

*————. ed. *The History of Childhood.* NY: The Psychohistory Press, 1974. Harper & Row Torchbook, 1975.

Demos, John. "Developmental perspectives on the History of Childhood." *The Journal of Interdisciplinary History* 2 (1971): 315-28. Also in *The Family in History.* Ed. by K. Rabb and Robert Rotberg. NY: Harper & Row, 1971.

*————. *A Little Commonwealth: Family Life in Plymouth Colony.* NY: Oxford Univ. Press, 1970.

———— and Demos, Virginia. "Adolescence in Historical Perspective." *Journal of Marriage and the Family* 31 (1969): 632-38.

Despert, Juliette Louise. *Children and War.* Washington, D.C., 1943.

————. *The Emotionally Disturbed Child—Then and Now.* NY: Robert Brunner, Inc., 1965.

————. *Preliminary Report on Children's Reaction to the War, Including a Critical Survey of the Literature.* NY, 1942.

Devereux, E. C., Bronfenbrenner, U. and Suci, G. J. "Patterns of Parent Behavior in the United States of America and the Federal Republic of Germany: A Cross-National Comparison." *International Social Science Journal* 14 (1962): 488-506.

Dolto, Francoise. "French and American Children as Seen by a French Child

Analyst." In *Childhood in Contemporary Cultures*. Ed. by Margaret Mead and Martha Wolfenstein. Chicago: The Univ. of Chicago Press, 1955.

Drake, T. G. H. "Infant Welfare Laws in France in the 18th Century." *Annals of Medical History* 7 (1935): 51.

———. "The Wet Nurse in France in the Eighteenth Century." *Bulletin of the History of Medicine* 8 (1940): 934-48.

Du Colombier, Cf. P. *L'enfant du Moyen Age*. Paris, 1951.

Duffy, John. "Masturbation and Clitoridectomy: A Nineteenth Century View." *Journal of the American Medical Association* 186 (1963): 246.

Dunlop, O. Jocelyn. *English Apprenticeship and Child Labour*. London, 1912.

Dunn, Dr. Courtenay. *The Natural History of the Child*. NY: John Lane, 1920.

Dunn, Patrick P. "That Enemy is the Baby: Childhood in Imperial Russia." In *The History of Childhood*. Ed by Lloyd deMause. NY: 1974.

Earle, Alice M. *Child Life in Colonial Days*. 1899 Reprint. Norwood, Pa., n.d.

———. *Home Life in Colonial Days*. NY: Macmillan, 1910.

Edwards, C. E. "Calvin on Infant Salvation." *Biblioteca Sacra* 88, 1931.

Elder, Glen H. Jr. *Children of the Great Depression: Social Structure and Personality*. Chicago: Univ. of Chicago Press, 1974.

Eng, Erling. "Cellini's Two Childhood Memories" *American Imago* 13 (1956): 189-203.

Erlanger, Howard C. "Social Class and Corporal Punishment in Children: A Reassessment." *American Sociological Review* 39 (1974): 68-85.

Esler, Anthony. *The Aspiring Mind of the Elizabethan Younger Generation*. Durham, N.C.: Duke Univ. Press, 1966.

———, ed. *The Youth Revolution: The Conflict of Generations in Modern History*. Lexington, Mass.: D. C. Heath, 1974. [With complete bibliography of youth movements.]

Étienne, R. "La Conscience Médicale Antique et la vie des Enfants." *Annales de Démographie Historique* (1973): 15-46.

Farber, Bernard. *Guardians of Virtue: Salem Families in 1800*. NY: Basic Books, 1972.

Field, E. M. *The Child and His Book*. London, 1892. Reprint, Detroit, 1968.

Findlay, Joseph J. *Children of England: A Contribution to Social History and to Education*. London, 1923.

Finkelstein, Barbara. "Pedagogy as Intrusion: Teaching Values in Popular Primary Schools in Nineteenth-Century America." *History of Childhood Quarterly* 2 (1975): 349-78.

Fisher, J. D. C. *Christian Initiation: Baptism in the Medieval West*. London, 1965.

Flandrin, Jean Louis. "L'attitude à l'égard du petit enfant et les conduites sexuelles dans la civilisation occidentale: Structures anciennes et évolution. *Annales de Démographie Historique* (1973): 143-210.

———. "Mariage tardif et vie sexuelle: Discussions et hypothéses de recherche." *Annales: Economies Societes Civilisations* 27 (1972): 1351-78.

Fleming, Sanford. *Children and Puritanism: The Place of Children in the Life and Thought of the New England Churches 1620-1847*. NY: Arno Press, 1969.

Fohlen, C. "Revolution industrielle et travail des enfants." *Annales de Demographie Historique* (1973): 319-25.

Foote, J. "An Infant Hygiene Campaign of the Second Century." *Archives of Pediatrics* 37 (1920): 181.

Freud, Anna and Burlingham, Dorothy. *War and Children*. NY: Intl. Univ. Press, 1943.

Frost, J. William. *The Quaker Family in Colonial America*. NY: St. Martin's Press, 1973.

Furnivall, F. J., ed. *Child Marriages, Divorces and Ratifications 1561-66*. Early English Text Society, Original Series. NY: Keans Reprint Co., 1897.

Gadoffre, Gilbert. "Conformisme et révolte dans la jeunesse allemande." *Psyché-Paris* 3 (1948): 834-43.

Gaines, David I. "Story of an English Cotton Mill Lad." *History of Childhood*

Quarterly 2 (1974): 249-64.

Ganiage. Jean. *Sur la Population francais au XVIII et au XIX siecles.* Paris: Societe de Demographie Historique, 1974.

Garland, Madge. *The Changing Face of Childhood.* NY: October House, 1965.

Garnier, F. L'iconographie de l'enfant au Moyen Age." *Annales de Démographie Historique* (1973): 135-36.

*Gathorne-Hardy, Jonathan. *The Rise and Fall of the British Nanny.* London: Hodder & Stoughton, 1973. Pub. in U.S. as *The Unnatural History of the Nanny.* NY: Dial Press, 1973.

Gauban, O. *De l'infanticide.* Bordeaux, 1905.

Geiger, H. Kent. *Family in Soviet Russia.* Cambridge, Mass.: Harvard Univ. Press, 1968.

Gibbs, Mary Ann. *The Years of the Nannies.* London: Hutchinson, 1960.

Glotz, G. *L'Exposition des enfants, études sociales et jurisdiques sur l'antiquité grecque.* Paris, 1906.

Godfrey, Elizabeth. *English Children in the Olden Time.* London, 1907.

———. *Home Life Under the Stuarts, 1603-1649.* NY: E. P. Dutton, 1904.

Goertzel, V. and Goertzel, M. G. *Cradles of Eminence.* Boston: Little, Brown, 1962.

Goode, William J. *World Revolution and Family Patterns.* NY: The Free Press, 1963.

Goodich, Michael. "Childhood and Adolescence Among the Thirteenth-Century Saints." *History of Childhood Quarterly* 1 (1973): 285-309.

Goodsell, Willystine. *A History of Marriage and The Family.* NY: 1934.

Gordon, Michael, ed. *The American Family in Social-Historical Perspective.* NY: St. Martin's Press, 1973.

Gorman, Sister Mary Rosaria. *The Nurse in Greek Life: A Dissertation.* Boston, 1917.

Gottlieb, David; Reeves, John; Tenn Houten, Warren. *The Emergence of Youth Societies: A Cross-Cultural Approach.* NY: 1966.

Goubert, Pierre. "Legitimate Fecundity and Infant Mortality in France During the Eighteenth Century: A Comparison." *Daedalus,* Spring, 1968.

Gouesse, J. M. "En Basse-Normandie aux XVIIe et XVIIIe siècles: le refus de l'enfant au tribunal de la pénitence." *Annales de Démographie Historique* (1973): 231-62.

Gouroff, A. *Essai sur l'histoire des enfants trouvés.* Paris, 1829.

Graff, H. J. "Patterns of Dependency and Child Development in the Mid-Nineteenth Century City: A Sample From Boston, 1860." *History of Education Quarterly* 13 (1973): 129-43.

*Greven, Philip J., Jr. *Child Rearing Concepts, 1628-1861.* Itasca, Ill., 1973.

Haffner, Carl. "The Changeling: History and Psychodynamics of Attitudes to Handicapped Children in European Folklore." *Journal of the History of the Behavioral Sciences* 4 no. 1 (1968): 55-61.

Hall, Stanley G. *Adolescence—Its Psychology and Its Relation to Physiology, Anthropology, Sociology, Sex, Crime, Religion and Education.* 2 vol. Reprint of 1905 ed. NY: Arno Press, 1970.

Handlin, Oscar. *Facing Life: Youth and the Family in American History.* Boston: Little, Brown & Co., 1971.

*Hare, E. H. "Masturbatory Insanity: The History of an Idea." *Journal of Mental Science* 108 (Jan., 1962).

Harris, Irving D. *The Promised Seed: A Comparative Study of Eminent First and Later Sons.* Glencoe: The Free Press, 1964.

Harrison, Molly. *Children in History.* 4 vol. Chester Springs, Pa.: Dufour, 1963.

Hartman, Mary S. "Child-Abuse and Self-Abuse: Two Victorian Cases." *History of Childhood Quarterly* 2 (1974): 221-48.

Hawes, Joseph M. *Children in Urban Society: Juvenile Delinquency in Nineteenth Century America.* Fair Lawn,N.J.: Oxford Univ. Press, Inc., 1971.

Hélin, E. "Une sollicitude ambiguë: l'évacuation des enfants abandonnés." *Annales de Démographie Historique* (1973): 225-30.

Heywood, James S. *Children in Care: The Development of the Services for the Deprived Child.* NY: Fernhill House Ltd., 1965.

Hildebrand, Harold N. *Child Actors: A Chapter in Elizabethan Stage History.* N.p.: Harold N. Hildebrand, 1964.

Hilgard, J. R.; Newman F.; Fisk, F. "Strength of Adult Ego Following Childhood Bereavement." *American Journal of Orthopsychiatry* 30 (1960): 788-98.

Hill, Reuben. *Families Under Stress: Adjustment to the Crisis of War Separation and Reunion.* Westport, Conn.: Greenwood Press, 1949.

Hoffman, Edith. *Children in the Past.* London, n.d.

Hole, Christina. *English Home-Life, 1500-1800.* London: Batsford, 1947.

———. *The English Housewife in the Seventeenth Century.* London, 1953.

Homan, Walter J. *Children and Quakerism.* NY: Arno Press, 1972.

Horn, Klaus. *Dressur oder Erziehung Schlagrituale und ihre gesselschaftliche Funktion.* Frankfurt am Main: Suhrkamp Verlag, 1970.

Hostetler, J. and Huntington, G. *Children in Amish Society: Socialization and Community Education.* NY: Holt, Rinehart & Winston, Inc.

Hügel, F. S. *Die Findelhäuser und das Findelwesen in Europa.* Vienna, 1863.

*Hunt, David. *Parents and Children in History.* NY: Basic Books, 1970.

Hurstfield, Joel. *The Queen's Wards: Wardship and Marriage Under Elizabeth I.* London: Longmans, Green & Co., 1958.

Hymanson, A. "A Short Review of the History of Infant Feeding." *Archives of Pediatrics* 51 (1934).

*Illick, Joseph E. "Child-Rearing in Seventeenth-Century England and America." In *The History of Childhood.* Ed. by Lloyd deMause. NY: Psychohistory Press, 1974.

Ironside, Charles E. *The Family in Colonial New York: A Sociological Study.* NY, 1942.

Jacoby, G. P. *Catholic Child Care in the Nineteenth Century.* Washington, D.C.: Catholic Univ. of America Press, 1941.

Janney, F. Lamar. *Childhood in English Non-Dramatic Literature From 1557 to 1798.* Dissertation. Johns Hopkins Univ., 1924. Grifswald, 1925.

Jeremias, J. *Infant Baptism in the First Four Centuries.* London, 1960.

———. *The Origins of Infant Baptism.* Naperville, Ill., n.d.

Josephson, E. *Political Youth Organization in Europe, 1900-1950.* Unpublished Ph.D. Thesis. Columbia Univ., 1959.

Karr, Ch. and Wesley, F. "Comparison of German and U.S. Child-Rearing Practices." *Child Development* 37 (1966): 715-23.

Kellum, Barbara A. "Infanticide in England in the Later Middle Ages." *History of Childhood Quarterly* 1 (1973): 367-88.

Keniston, Kenneth. *The Uncommitted: Alienated Youth in American Society.* NY: Dell Publishing, 1970.

———. "Youth: A 'New' Stage of Life." *American Scholar* 39 (1970: 631-54.

Kern, Stephen. "Explosive Intimacy: Psychodynamics of the Victorian Family." *History of Childhood Quarterly* 1 (1973): 437-61.

Kessen, William. *The Child.* NY: John Wiley & Sons, 1965.

Kett, Joseph F. "Adolescence and Youth in Nineteenth-Century America." *The Journal of Interdisciplinary History* 2 (1971): 283-99.

———. "Growing Up in Rural New England, 1800-1840." In *Anonymous Americans.* Ed. by T. K. Hareven. Englewood Cliffs, 1971.

Kiefer, Monica. *American Children Through Their Books, 1700-1835.* Phila.: 1948.

———. "Early American Childhood in the Middle Atlantic Area." *Pennsylvania Magazine of History and Biography* 68 (1944).

King-Hall, Magdalen. *The Story of the Nursery.* London: Routledge & Kegan Paul, 1958.

Klapisch, C. "L'enfance en Toscane au début du XVe siécle." *Annales de Demographie Historique* (1973): 99-120.

Klein, Anita. *Child Life in Greek Art.* NY: Columbia Univ. Press, 1932.

Kossak, Margaretha. "Sexuelle Verführung der Kinder durch Diensten." *Sexualprobleme,* 1913.

Lacey, W. K. *The Family in Classical Greece.* Ithaca, N.Y.: Cornell U. Press, 1968.
Lallemand, Leon. *Histoire des enfants abandonnés et délaissés.* Paris, 1885.
Langer, William L. "Checks on Population Growth: 1750-1850." *Scientific American* (1972): 93-99.
*———. "Infanticide: A Historical Survey." *History of Childhood Quarterly* 1 (1973): 353-67; 2 (1974): 129-34.
La Rue Van Hook. "The Exposure of Infants at Athens." *American Philological Association Transactions and Proceedings* 51 (1920): 36-44.
Laslett, Peter, "L'attitude a l'egard de l'enfant dans l' Angleterre du XIX siècle d'apres les sources litteraires, politiques et jurisdiques." *Annales de Demographie Historique* (1973): 313-18.
———, ed. *Household and Family in Past Time.* Cambridge: Cambridge Univ. Press, 1972.
———. *The World We Have Lost: England Before the Industrial Age.* NY: 1965.
Lebrun, Francois. "Naissances illegitimes et abandons d'enfants au XVIIIe siecle." *Annales: Economies, Societees, Civilisations* 27 (1972).
Lefebvre, O. *La famille en France dans le droit et dans le moeurs.* Paris, 1920.
Le Fort L. "De la mortalite des enfants et de l'industrie des nourrices en France." *Revue des Deux Mondes,* March 15, 1870.
Legasse, Cf. C. *Jésus et l'enfant. Enfants, petits et simples dans la tradition synoptique.* Paris, 1964.
Le Goff, J. "Petits enfants dans la littérature des XIIe-XIIIe siècles." *Annales de Demographie Historique* (1973): 129-32.
Legouvé, E. *Les Pères et les Enfants au XIX siecle.* Paris, n.d.
Lehnhoff, Wilhelm. *Spiele und Streiche aus den Kindheitstagen der Dichter und Meister.* Leipzig: Brandstetter, n.d.
Le Vine, Robert A.; Klein, Nancy H.; and Owen, Constance F. "Modernization and father-child relationships." In *A Modern Introduction to the Family.* Ed. by Norman W. Bell and Ezra F. Vogel. NY: The Free Press, 1968.
Levinson, Abraha. *Pioneers of Pediatrics.* NY: Froben Press, 1943.
Lipton, Earle L.; Steinschneider, Alfred; Richmond, Julius B. "Swaddling, a Child Care Practice: Historical, Cultural and Experimental Observations." *Pediatrics* 35 (1965): 521-67.
Lochhead, Marion. *Their First Ten Years: Victorian Childhood.* London, 1956.
Lopez, Manuel D. "A Guide to the Interdisciplinary Literature of the History of Childhood." *History of Childhood Quarterly* 1 (1974): 463-94.
Lorence, Bogna W. "Parents and Children in Eighteenth Century Europe." *History of Childhood Quarterly* 2 (1974): 1-30.
Lumpkin, Katherine D. and Douglas, Dorothy W. *Child Workers in America.* N.p.: Books For Libraries, 1937.
Lyman, Richard B. Jr. "Barbarism and Religion: Late Roman and Early Medieval Childhood." In *The History of Childhood.* Ed. by Lloyd deMause. NY: The Psychohistory Press, 1974.

McCleary, George F. *The Maternity and Child Welfare Movement.* London, 1935.
McClinton, Katherine Morrison. *Antiques of American Childhood.* NY: Bramhall House, 1970.
McCurdy, Harold. "The Childhood Pattern of Genius." *Horizon* 2 (1960): 33-38.
McDaniel, Walton B. *Conception, Birth and Infancy in Ancient Rome and Modern Italy.* Coconut Grove, Florida, 1948.
MacFarlane, Alan. *The Family Life of Ralph Josselin, A Seventeenth-Century Clergyman.* Cambridge: Cambridge Univ. Press, 1970.
McLaughlin, Mary Martin. "Survivors and Surrogates: Children and Parents From the Ninth to the Thirteenth Centuries." In *The History of Childhood.* Ed. by Lloyd deMause. NY: The Psychohistory Press, 1974.

Macquoid, Percy. *Four Hundred Years of Children's Costumes From the Great Masters, 1400-1800.* London: The Medici Society, 1923.
Madison, Bernice. "Russia's Illegitimate Children." *Slavic Review* XXII (1963): 82-95.
March, Hans. "Sexuelle Konflikte in den Reifejahren." (Onanie). *Psyche, Zehlendorf,* 1949, 30 p.

Mare, Walter de la. *Early One Morning in the Spring: Chapters on Children and on Childhood.* London: Faber and Faber, 1935.

Margolius, A. *Mutter und Kind im Altbiblischen Schrifttum.* Berlin, 1936.

Marples, Morris. *Princes in the Making.* London: Faber and Faber, 1965.

Marrou, H. I. *A History of Education in Antiquity.* NY: 1956.

Martin, L. C. "Henry Vaughan and the Theme of Infancy." In *Seventeenth Century Studies Presented to Sir Herbert Grierson.* Oxford, 1938.

*Marvick, Elizabeth Wirth. "Nature Versus Nurture: Patterns and Trends in Seventeenth Century French Child-Rearing." In *The History of Childhood.* Ed. by Lloyd deMause. NY: The Psychohistory Press, 1974.

Mayer, Henry. "From Young Man to Adolescent: Social Control and the Concept of Adolescence 1880-1905," paper read at the annual convention of the American Historical Association, Dec. 29, 1971, at New York, N.Y.

Mead, Margaret and Wolfenstein, Martha. *Childhood in Contemporary Cultures.* Chicago, 1966.

Mercier, Roger. *L'enfant dans la societe du XVIIIe siecle.* Universite de Dakar, Faculte des Lettres et Sciences Humaine. Dakar, 1951.

Metraux, Rhoda. "Parents and Children: An Analysis of Contemporary German Child-Care and Youth-Guidance Literature." In *Childhood in Contemporary Cultures.* Ed. by Margaret Mead and Martha Wolfenstein. Chicago: The Univ. of Chicago Press, 1955.

Miller, Daniel R. and Swanson, Guy E. *The Changing American Parent: A Study in the Detroit Area* NY: Wiley & Sons, 1958.

Mogen, John M. "A Century of Declining Parental Authority." *Marriage and Family Living* 19 (1957): 234-39.

Moller, Herbert. "Youth as a Force in the Modern World." *Comparative Studies in Society and History* X (1968): 237-60.

Morgan, Edmund S. *The Puritan Family: Religion and Domestic Relations in Seventeenth-Century New England* (Rev. ed., NY: 1966).

———. *Virginians at Home: Family Life in the Eighteenth Century.* Williamsburg: Colonial Williamsburg, 1952.

Nichols, R. H. and Wray, F. H. *The History of the Founding Hospital.* London, 1935.

Niedzielski, Zygmunt. *The Athenian Family from Aeschylus to Aristotle.* Doctoral Dissertation. Univ. of Chicago, 1955.

O'Brien, Edward J. *Child Welfare Legislation in Maryland, 1634-1936.* Washington, D.C.: The Catholic Univ. of America Press, 1937.

Olden, Christine. "Notes on Child Rearing in America." *The Psychoanalytic Study of the Child* 7, 1952.

Parker, Clifford Stetson. *The Defense of the Child by French Novelists.* Menasha, Wisc.: George Banta Publishing, 1925.

Patlagean, C. "L'Enfant et son avenir dans la famille byzantine." *Annales de Démographie Historique* (1973): 85-94.

*Payne, George H. *The Child in Human Progress.* Ann Arbor, Mich: Finch Press, 1916.

*Peiper, Albrecht. *Chronik der Kinderheilkunde.* Leipzig, 1966.

———. *Quellen zur Geschichte der Kinderheilkunde, zus ammengestellt, eingeleitet und kommentiert von Albrecht Peiper.* Bern: Humber, 1966.

Pentikainen, Juha, *The Nordic Dead-Child Traditions.* Helsinki, 1968.

*Pinchbeck, Ivy and Hewitt, Margaret. *Children in English Society.* Vol. I—From Tudor Times to Eighteenth Century. Vol. II—From the Eighteenth Century to the Children's Act 1848. Buffalo, N.Y': University of Toronto Press, 1970, and London: Routledge & Kegan Paul, 1973.

Pinchbeck, Joy. "The State and the Child in Sixteenth Century England." *British Journal of Sociology* 7 (1956): 273-85; 8 (1957): 59-74.

Piponnier, F. "Les Objets de l'enfance." *Annales de Demographie Historique* (1973): 69-72.

Plant, Margorie. *The Domestic Life of Scotland in the Eighteenth Century.* Edinburgh: University Press, 1952.

Platt, Anthony M. *The Child Savers: The Invention of Delinquency.* Chicago: The Univ. of Chicago Press, 1969.

Post, L. A. "Dramatic Infants in Greek." *Classical Philology* 34, 1939.

Powell, Chilton Latham. *English Domestic Relations, 1487-1653.* NY: Columbia Univ. Press, 1917.

Rabb, Theodore K. and Rotberg, Robert, eds. *The Family in History: Interdisciplinary Essays.* NY: Harper & Row, 1971.

Rabbie, J. M. "A Cross-Cultural Comparison of Parent-Child Relationships in the United States and West Germany." *The British Journal of Social and Clinical Psychology* 4 no. 4 (1965): 298-310.

Radbill, Samuel X. "A History of Child Abuse and Infanticide." In *The Battered Child.* Chicago: The Univ. of Chicago Press, 1968.

Raden, Max. "Exposure of Infants in Roman Law and Practice." *Classical Journal* 20 (1925): 342-43.

Raichle, Donald R. "The Abolition of Corporal Punishment in New Jersey Schools." *History of Childhood Quarterly* 2 (1974): 53-78

Rapson, Richard. "The American Child as Seen by British Travellers, 1845-1935." *American Quarterly* XVIII (1965): 520-34.

Remacle, Bernard. *Des hospices des enfants trouvés en Europe, et principalement en France.* Paris, 1838.

Rendle-Short, John and Rendle-Short, Rowena. *Father of Child Care: The Life of William Cadogan, 1711-1797.* Briston: John Wright and Sons, Ltd., 1966.

Rendle-Short, John. "Infant Management in the Eighteenth Century With a Special Reference to the Work of William Cadogan." *Bulletin of the History of Medicine* XXXIV no. 2 (March-April, 1960).

Renouard, Yves. "La notion de génération en histoire." *Revue historique* 260 (1953): 1-23.

Riché, Pierre. "L'enfant dans le haut Moyen Age." *Annales de Demographie Historique* (1973): 95-98.

———. "L'enfant dans la société monastique au XII⁰ siècle." In *Actes du Colloque de Cluny,* 1972.

———. "L'enfant dans la société monastique aux XI⁰ et XII⁰ siècles." *Actes, Colloque international, Pierre Abélard-Pierre le Vénérable.* Paris, 1974.

Robertson, Priscilla. "Home As a Nest: Middle Class Childhood in Nineteenth-Century Europe." In *The History of Childhood.* Ed. by Lloyd deMause. NY: The Psychohistory Press, 1974.

Rodgers, R. R. "Changes in Parental Behavior Reported by Children in West Germany and the United States." *Human Development* 14 (1971): 208-24.

Roe, Frederick Gordon. *The Georgian Child.* London, 1961.

———. *The Victorian Child.* London, 1959.

Roller, Bert. *Children in American Poetry, 1610-1900.* Nashville, 1930.

Ross, Helen. "Children in Wartime." *Junior League Magazine,* Oct., 1941.

Ross, J. B. "The Middle-Class Child in Urban Italy, Fourteenth to Early Sixteenth Century" in *The History of Childhood,* Lloyd deMause, ed. NY: The Psychohistory Press, 1974.

Rothman, David J. "Documents in Search of a Historian: Toward a History of Childhood and Youth in America." In *The Family in History.* Ed. by Theodore K. Rabb and Robert Rotberg. NY: Harper & Row, 1971.

——— and Sheila Rothman, eds. *The Colonial American Family: Collected Essays.* NY: The Arno Press, 1972.

Royaume de Belgique. Ministere de l'Intérieur. *Enquéte sur la condition des classes ouvrières et sur le travail des enfants.* Brussels, 1846-1848.

*Ruhrah, John, comp. & ed. *Pediatrics of the Past: An Anthology Compiled and Edited . . .* NY: Paul B. Hoeber, 1925.

Rusk, Robert R. *A History of Infant Education.* London: Univ. of London Press, 1951.

Ryan, William Burke. *Infanticide: Its Law, Prevalence, Prevention, and History.* London: J. Churchill, 1862.

Ryerson, Alice Judson. *Medical Advice on Child Rearing, 1650-1900.* Unpubl. Harvard Thesis, 1960.

Sanders, Wiley B. ed. *Juvenile Offenders For a Thousand Years.* Selected Readings From Anglo-Saxon Times to 1900. Chapel Hill: Univ. of N. Carolina, 1970.

*Sangster, Paul. *Pity My Simplicity.* London: Epsworth Press, 1963.

Santiago, Luciano C. *Children of Oedipus: Brother and Sister Incest in Psychiatry, Literature, History and Mythology.* Roslyn Heights, L.I.: Libra Publishers, Inc., 1973.

Saveth, Edward N. "The Problem of American Family History." *American Quarterly* 21 (1969): 311-29.

Schattner, B. *Father Land: A Study of Authoritarianism in the German Family.* NY: Columbia Univ. Press, 1948.

*Schatzman, Morton. *Soul Murder: Persecution in the Family.* NY: Random House, 1973.

Schnucker, R. V. "The English Puritans and Pregnancy, Delivery and Breast Feeding." *History of Childhood Quarterly* 1 (1974): 637-658.

Schucking, Levin L. *The Puritan Family: A Social Study From the Literary Sources.* NY: 1970.

Scudder, Horace E. *Childhood in Literature and Art.* Boston: Houghton, Mifflin, 1894.

Sears, Robert R., et al. *Patterns of Child Rearing.* NY: Harper & Row, 1957.

Sémichon, E. *Histoire des enfants abandonnés depuis l'Antiquite jusq'a nos jours: le tour.* Paris, 1880, 344 p.

Seth, Ronald. *Children Against Witches.* London: Robert Hale, 1969.

Shepherd, Katheleen K. *Better Unborn Than Untaught: Sixteenth-Century Popular Advice on Child Rearing in England.* Columbia Univ. Master's Thesis, 1965.

Shorter, Edward. "Infanticide in the Past." *History of Childhood Quarterly* 1 (1973): 178-80.

Skolnick, Arlene S. and Jerome H. *Family in Transition: Rethinking Marriage, Sexuality, Child Rearing and Family Organization.* Boston: Little, Brown, 1971.

Silverman, Henry J. "Youth of the 1930s and the 1960s," paper read at the annual convention of the American Historical Association, Dec. 28, 1973, at San Francisco, Calif.

Simeral, Isabel. *Reform Movement in Behalf of Children in England of the Early Nineteenth Century, and the Agents of Those Reforms.* Clifton, N.J., 1971.

Slater, Peter G. *Child Rearing Practices in New England, Late Eighteenth, Early Nineteenth Centuries.* Doctoral Dissertation. U.C. Berkeley, 1971.

Smith, Steven R. "Religion and the Conception of Youth in Seventeenth-Century England." *History of Childhood Quarterly* 2 (1975): 493-516. ·

Sommerville, John C. "Towards a History of Childhood and Youth." *Journal of Interdisciplinary History* 3 (1972): 438-447.

Sous, G. *Histoire des enfants trouvés de Bordeaux.* Bordeaux, 1865.

*Spitz, Rene A. "Authority and Masturbation: Some Remarks on Bibliographical Investigation." *The Psychoanalytic Quarterly* 21, 1952.

———. "Frünkindliches Erleben und Erwachsenkultur bein den Primitiven." *Imago* 21 (1935): 367-87.

Spitzer, Alan. "The Historical Problem of Generations." *American Historical Review* 78 (1973): 1353-85.

Steere, Geoffrey H. "Freudianism and Child Rearing in the Twenties." *American Quarterly* 10 (1968): 759-67.

Stern, Bernhard J. *Family, Past and Present.* Ann Arbor, Mich.: Finch Press, 1938.

Stern, Erich. "L'enfant de la maison d'enfants. Essai Psychologique." *Zeitschrift für Kinderpsychiatrie* 16 (1949): 17-24; 33-43.

Stickland, Irina, comp. *The Voices of Children 1700-1914.* NY: Barnes & Noble, 1973.

*Still, George. *History of Pediatrics.* London: Dawson of Pall Mall, 1953.

Stolz, Lois Meel, et al. *Father Relations of War-Born Children.* NY: Greenwood Press, 1968.

Stone, Lawrence. "The Massacre of the Innocents." *New York Review of Books* (Nov. 14, 1974): 25-31.

Stone, Michael H. "The History of Child Psychiatry Before the Twentieth Century." *International Journal of Child Psychotherapy* 2 (1973): 264-308.

———. "Mesmer and His Followers: The Beginnings of Sympathetic Treatment of

Childhood Emotional Disorders." *History of Childhood Quarterly* 1 (1974): 659-80.
―――― and Kestenbaum, Clarice. "Maternal Deprivation in Children of the Wealthy: A Paradox in Socioeconomic vs. Psychological Class." *History of Childhood Quarterly* 2 (1974): 79-106.
Strickland, Charles. "A Transcendentalist Father: The Child-rearing Practices of Bronson Alcott." *History of Childhood Quarterly* 1 (1973): 4-51.
Strong, Bryan. "Ideas of the Early Sex Education Movement in America, 1890-1920." *History of Education Quarterly* 12 (1972): 129-61.
Stuart, Dorothy M. *Child's Day Through the Ages.* Ann Arbor, Mich.: Finch, 1941.
Sudhoff, Karl. *Erstlinge der pädiatrischen Literatur.* Munich, 1925.
Sunley, Robert. "Early Nineteenth-Century American Literature on Child Rearing. In *Childhood in Contemporary Cultures.* Ed. by Margaret Mead and Martha Wolfenstein. Chicago: The Univ. of Chicago Press, 1955.

Tamm, Alfhild. "Die Eltern und die Onanie ihrer Kinder." *Zeitschrift für psychoanalytische Pädagogik* 2 (1927-28): 187-88.
*Taylor, Gordon Rattray. The Angel-Makers: *A Study in the Psychological Origins of Historical Change. 1750-1850.* London: William Heinemann, 1958.
Tenenti, A. "Temoignages toscans sur la mort des enfants autour de 1400." *Annales de Démographie Historique* (1973): 133-34.
Terme, J., and Monfalcon, J. B. *Histoire des enfants trouvés.* Paris, 1840.
Thirsk, Joan. "Younger Sons in the Seventeenth Century." *History* LIV (1969): 359-77.
Thrupp, John. *The Anglo-Saxon Home: A History of the Domestic Institutions and Customs of England. From the Fifth to the Eleventh Century.* London, 1862.
Tilly, Charles. "Population and Pedagogy in France." *History of Education Quarterly* 13 (1973): 113-28.
Tobey, James A. *Children's Bureau: Activities and Organization.* Reprint of 1925 ed. NY: AMS Press Inc., n.d.
Toledano, A. D. *La vie de famille sous la Restauration et la Monarchie de Juillet.* Paris, 1943.
Tolley, Howard B., Jr. *Children and War: Political Socialization in International Conflict.* NY: Teachers College Press, Columbia Univ., 1973.
Toursch, V. *L'enfant français à la fin du XIXe siècle, d'apres ses principaux romanciers.* Paris, 1939.
Trattner, Walter I. *Crusade for the Children: A History of the National Child Labor Committee and Child Labor Reform in America.* Chicago, 1970.
Trexler, Richard. "Infanticide in Florence." *History of Childhood Quarterly* 1 (1973): 98-117.
―――――. "The Foundlings of Florence, 1395-1455." *History of Childhood Quarterly* 1 (1973): 259-84.
Tucker, M. J. "The Child as Beginning and End: Fifteenth and Sixteenth Century English Childhood." In *The History of Childhood.* Ed. by Lloyd deMause. NY: The Psychohistory Press, 1974.

Vann, Richard T. "Nurture and Conversion in the Early Quaker Family." *Journal of Marriage and the Family* 31 (1969): 639-43.
Valentine, Alan, Ed. *Fathers and Sons: Advice Without Consent.* Norman: Univ. of Oklahoma Press, 1963.

Walle, Etienne van de. "Recent Approaches to Past Childhoods." In *The Family in History.* Ed. by Theodore K. Rabb and Robert Rotberg. NY: Harper & Row, 1971.
*Walzer, John F. "A Period of Ambivalence: Eighteenth Century American Childhood." In *The History of Childhood.* Ed. by Lloyd deMause. NY: The Psychohistory Press, 1974.
Waters, Elinor and Vaughn J. Crandall. "Social Class and Observed Maternal Behavior from 1940 to 1960." In *Readings in the Psychology of Parent-Child Relations.* Ed. by Gene R. Medinnus. NY: Wiley & Sons, 1967.

Weber-Kellermann, Ingeborg. *Die Deutsche Familie Versuch einer Sozialgeschichte.* Frankfurt: Suhrkamp Verlag, 1974.

Wechssler, Eduard. *Die Generation als Jugendreihe und Ihr Kampf um die Denkform.* Leipzig, 1930.

Werner, Oscar H. *The Unmarried Mother in German Literature.* NY: AMS Press, 1966.

Whitebread, Nanette. *The Evolution of the Nursery-Infant School.* London: Routledge and Kegan Paul, 1972.

White, Morton, S. "Social Class, Child Rearing Practices, and Child Behavior." *American Sociological Review* 22 (1957): 704-12.

Whiting, John W. M. and Child, Irwin L. *Child Training and Personality: A Cross-Cultural Study.* New Haven, 1953.

Wickes, Ian. "A History of Infant Feeding." *Archives of Disease in Childhood* XXVIII (1935): 232.

Wilson, Elizabeth A. *Hygienic Care and Management of the Child in the American Family Prior to 1860.* Duke Univ. Master's Thesis, 1940.

Winnik, Heinrich Z. and Horovitz, M. "The Problem of Infanticide." *British Journal of Criminology* 2 (1961): 40-52.

Wishy, Bernard. *The Child and the Republic.* Philadelphia: Univ. of Penn. Press, 1972.

Wolfenstein, Martha. "Fun Morality: An Analysis of Recent American Child-Training Literature." In *Childhood in Contemporary Cultures.* Ed. by Margaret Mean and Martha Wolfenstein. Chicago: Chicago Univ. Press, 1955.

Wood, Robert. *Children 1773-1890.* NY: International Publ. Service, 1968.

Zander, Alfred. "Onaniebekämpfung vor 120 Jahren." *Zeitschrift für psychoanalytische Pädagogik* 5 (1931): 465-66.

III. ANCIENT

Abraham, Karl. "Amenhotep IV (Ikhnaton): A Psychoanalytic Contribution to the Understanding of His Personality and the Monotheistic Cult of Ahn." *Psychoanalytic Quarterly* 4 (1935): 537-69.

Allwohn, A. *Die Ehe des Propheten Hosea in Psychoanalytischer Beleuchtung.* Giessen: A. Töpelman, 1926.

Bakan, David. "Moses in the Thought of Freud: An Ambivalent Interpretation," *Commentary* 26 (1958): 322-31.

Barag, Gerda. "The Mother in the Religious Concepts of Judaism." *American Imago* 4 (1946): 32-53.

Beck, Samuel J. "Abraham's Ordeal: Creation of a New Reality." *The Psychoanalytic Review* 50, 1963.

Berguer, Georges. *Some Aspects of the Life of Jesus From the Psychological and Psychoanalytical Point of View.* NY: Harcourt Brace, 1923.

Boven, William. "Alexander der Grosse." *Imago* 8 (1922): 418-39.

*Bradley, Noel. "Primal Scene Experiences in Human Evolution and Its Phantasy Derivatives in Art, Proto-Science and Philosophy." *The Psychoanalytic Study of Society* 4, 1967.

*———. "The Vulture as Mother Symbol: A Note on Freud's Leonardo." *American Imago* 22, 1965.

Bronner, Augusta Fox. "Psychiatric Concepts of the Early Greek Philosophers." *American Journal of Orthopsychiatry* 2 (1932): 103-13.

Brown, Norman O. "Rome—A Psychoanalytical Study." *Arethusa* 7 (1974): 95-101.

Bunker, Henry A. "The Bouphonia, or Ox-Murder: A Footnote to Totem and Taboo." *Psychoanalysis and the Social Sciences* I, 1947: 165-69.

Bychowski, Gustav. "Julius Caesar and the Death of the Republic." *Journal of Clinical Psychopathology* 7 (1946): 679-96.

Cárcamo, Celes Ernesto. "La Serpiente Emplumada; Psichoanalisis de la Religion Maya-Azteca y del Sacrificio Humano." *Revista de Psichoanalisis,* Buenos Aires, I (1943): 5-38.

Clark, L. Pierce. "A Psychohistorical Study of Akhnaton, First Idealist and Originator of a Monotheistic Religion." *Archives of Psychoanalysis* 1 (1927): 241-254.

———. "A Psychohistorical Study of the Sex Balance in Greek Art." *Medical Journal and Rec.* 20, Feb. 6, 1924.

———. "Unconscious Motives Underlying the Personalities of Great Statesmen and Their Relation to Epoch-Making Events: The Narcism of Alexander the Great." *Psychoanalytic Review* 10 (1923): 56-69.

Coriat, Isadore Henry. "Totemism in Prehistoric Man." *Psychoanalytic Review* 21 (1934): 40-48.

Desmonde, William H. "The Bull-Fight as a Religious Ritual." *American Imago* 9, 1952.

———. "Compulsive Aspects of Ancient Law." *American Imago* 11 (1954): 85-110.

———. "The Murder of Moses." *Abs. Review* 41 (1954): 374-75.

———. "The Origin of Money in the Animal Sacrifice." *Journal of Hillside Hospital* 6 (1957): 7-23.

Deutsch, Helene. *A Psychoanalytic Study of the Myth of Dionysus and Apollo: Two Variants of the Son-Mother Relationship.* NY: International Press, 1969.

Devereux, George. "Belief, Superstition and Symptom." *Samiksa* 8 (1954): 210-15.

———. "La psychoanalyse et l'histoire: une application à l'histoire de Sparte." *Annales* 20 (1965): 18-44.

———. "Sociopolitical Functions of the Oedipus Myth in Early Greece." *The Psychoanalytic Quarterly* 32, 1963.

Dimont, M. I. *Jews, God and History.* NY: New American Library, 1962.

Dittes, James E. "Continuities Between the Life and Thought of Augustine." *Journal for the Scientific Study of Religion* 5 (1965-6): 130-40.

Dodds, E. R. *The Greeks and the Irrational.* Berkeley: Univ. of Cal. Press, 1964.

———. *Pagan and Christian in an Age of Anxiety.* Cambridge: Univ. of Cambridge, 1965.

Dover, K. J. "Classical Greek Attitudes to Sexual Behavior." *Arethusa* VI (1973): 59-74.

Dreifuss, Gustav. "Isaac, The Sacrificial Lamb: A Study of Some Jewish Legends." *Journal of Analytic Psychology* 16 (1971): 69-78.

Engle, Bernice S. "The Amazons in Ancient Greece." *Psychoanalytic Quarterly* 11 (1942): 512-54.

Engle, B. and French, T. "Some Psychodynamic Reflections Upon the Life and Writings of Solon." *Psychoanalytic Quarterly* 20 (1951): 253-74.

Feldman, Arthur A. "The Davidic Dynasty and the Davidic Messiah." *American Imago* 17 (1960): 163-178.

Feldman, Sandor S. "The Sin of Reuben, Firstborn Son of Jacob." In *Psychoanalysis and the Social Sciences* 4, pp. 282-287. Ed. by W. Muensterberger and S. Axelrod. New York, 1955.

Freeman, Derek. "Totem and Taboo: A Reappraisal." *The Psychoanalytic Study of Society* 4, 1967, pp. 9-33.

*Freud, Sigmund. *Moses and Monotheism.* Standard Edition, Vol. 23, pp. 7-269.

Fromm, Erich. "The Oedipus Complex and the Oedipus Myth." In *The Family: Its Functions and Destiny.* Ed. by R. N. Anshen. NY: Harper & Bros., 1949.

———. "Der Sabbath." *Imago* 13 (1927): 223-34. Reprinted in *The Forgotten Language,* 1951, pp. 241-49.

———. "Dauernde Nachwirkung eines Erziehungsfehlers." *Zeitschrift für Psychoanalytische Pädagogik* 10 (1927): 372-73.

———. "Robert Briffault's Werk über das Mutterrecht." *Zeitschrift für Sozialforschung* 2 (1933): 382-87.

———. "Die Sozialpsychologische Bedeutung der Muterrechtstheorie." *Zeitschrift für Sozialforschung* 3 (1934): 196-227. Published in English in *The Crisis of Psychoanalysis,* 1970.

Gomperz, Heinrich. "Psychologische Beobachtungen an griechischen Philosophen." *Imago* 10 (1924): 1-92.

Halpern, Sidney. "The Mother-Killer." *The Psychoanalytic Review* 52, 1965.
Hofling, Charles K. "Notes on Raychandhuri's 'Jesus Christ and Sree Kisna.' " *American Imago* 15 (1958): 213-26.

Isaac-Edersheim, E. (Messias, Golem, Ahasver; drei mytische Gestalten des Judentums.) I. "The Messiah." *Internationale Zeitschrift für ärtzliche Psychoanalyse* 26 (1941): 50-80. II. "The Golem." *Internationale Zeitschrift etc.* 26 (1941): 179-213. III. "The Wandering Jew." *Internationale Zeitschrift etc.* 26 (1941): 286-315.

Jelgersma, H. C. "Der Kannibalismus und seine Verdrängung in Alten Ägypten." *Imago* 14 (1928): 275-92.
Jenichen, Richard. "Über den Alptraum in der sächsischen Sagenwelt." *Zentralblatt für Psychoanalyse und Psychotherapie* 4 (1914): 481-85.
Jones, Ernest. "Moses and Monotheism." *International Journal of Psycho-Analysis* 21 (1940): 230-240.
June, Carl Gustav, *Essays on a Science of Mythology: The Myth of the Divine Child and the Mysteries of Eleusis.* NY: Pantheon Books, 1949.

Kaplan, Leo. "The Baal Schem Legend." *Psyche and Eros* 2 (1921): 173-83.
Karpas, Morris J. "Socrates in the Light of Modern Psychopathology." *Journal of Abnormal Psychology* 10 (1915): 185.
Kluckhohn, Clyde. "Recurrent Themes in Myths and Mythmaking." *Daedalus* 88 (1959): 268-79.

Laughlin, Henry P. "King David's Anger." *The Psychoanalytic Quarterly* 23 (1954): 87-95.
*Lederer, Wolfgang. *The Fear of Women.* New York: Greene & Stratton, 1968.
Leeuwe, Jules de. "Über die Entstehung religiöser Vorstellungen." *Internationale Zeitschrift für ärtzliche Psychoanalyse* 25 (1940: 430-443.
Leipolt, Johannes. *Die Frau in der antiken Welt und im Ur-Christentum.* Berlin, 1962.
Leschnitzer, Adolf F. "Faust and Moses." *American Imago* 6 (1949): 229-43.
Levin, A. J. "Oedipus and Sampson, the Rejected Hero-Child." *International Journal of Psycho-Analysis* 38, 1957.
Levin, Max. "Psychoanalytic Interpretation of Two Statements From the Talmud." *International Journal of Psycho-Analysis* 11 (1930): 94-95.
Lorenz, Emil Franz. "Die Träume des Pharao, des Mundschenken und des Bäckers." *Psychoanalytische Bewegung* 2 (1930): 33-45.

McConnell, U. H. "The Symbol in Legend." *Psyche* 13 (1933): 94-137.
Malev, Milton. "The Jewish Orthodox Circumcision Ceremony." *Journal of the American Psychoanalytic Association* 14, 1966.
Meier, Carl Alfred. "The Dream in Ancient Greece and Its Use in Temple Cures (Incubation)." In *The Dreams and Human Societies.* Ed. by G. Greenbaum and R. von Caillois. Berkeley/Los Angeles: Univ. of Calif. Press, 1966.
More, Joseph. "The Prophet Jonah: The Story of an Intrapsychic Process." *American Imago* 27 (Spring, 1970): 3-11.

O'Meara, John J. *Young Augustine.* Staten Island, N.Y.: Alba House, 1965.

Peto, Andrew. "The Demonic Mother Imago in the Jewish Religion." *Psychoanalysis and the Social Sciences,* 1958.

———. "The Development of Ethical Monotheism." *The Psychoanalytic Study of Society* I, 1960.
Pruyser, Paul W. "Psychological Examination: Augustine." *Journal for the Scientific Study of Religion* 5 (1965-6): 284-89.

Rank, Otto. *Myth of the Birth of the Hero and Other Essays*. NY: Random House, 1959.

*Reik, Theodor. *Myth and Guilt: The Crime and Punishment of Mankind*. NY: George Braziller, Inc., 1957.

———. *Pagan Rites in Judaism: From Sex Initiation, Magic, Mooncult, Tattooing, Mutilation, and other Primitive Rituals to Family Loyalty and Solidarity*. New York: Farrar Straus, 1964.

———. *Ritual: Psycho-Analytic Studies*. NY: International Univ. Press, 1946.

Roheim, Geza. *Animism, Magic and the Divine King*. London, Kegan Paul, 1930.

———. "The Covenant of Abraham." *International Journal of Psycho-Analysis* 20 (1939): 452-59.

———. "Cu-Chulainn and the Origin of Totemism." *Man* 25 (1925): 85-88.

———. *The Riddle of the Sphinx*. London: Hogarth Press, 1934.

———. "Some Aspects of Semitic Monotheism." *Psychoanalysis and the Social Sciences* 4, 1955.

*Sachs, Hans. "The Delay of the Machine Age." *The Psychoanalytic Quarterly* 2 (1933): 404-24.

Sarnoff, Charles A. "Mythic Symbols in Two Precolumbian Myths." *American Imago* 26 no. 1 (1969): 3-20.

Saussure, Raymond de. *Le Miracle Grec. Étude Psychoanalytique sur la Civilisation Hellénique*. Paris: Denöel, 1939.

Schestow, Leo. "Alexander und Diogenes." *Almanach* (1931): 117-119.

Schirren, Julius. "Das Archaion. Die Frage nach dem Geist." *Psyche* 2 (1948): 284-94.

Schneiderman, Leo. "The Death of Apsyrtus." *The Psychoanalytic Review* 54, 1967.

Schneiter, C. "Ein Traum Julius Caesars." *Zentralblatt für Psychoanalyse und Psychotherapie* 3 (1913): 557.

Segal, B. "Serpent-Staffs of Antiquity." *Hebrew Medical Journal* 2 (1963): 229-31.

Seidenberg, Robert. "Sacrificing the First You See." *The Psychoanalytic Review* 53 (1966): 52-60.

Sillman, Leonar R. "Monotheism and the Sense of Reality." *International Journal of Psycho-Analysis* 30 (1949): 124-32.

*Slater, Philip E. *The Glory of Hera: Greek Mythology and the Greek Family*. Boston: Beacon Press, 1968.

———. "The Greek Family in History and Myth." *Arethusa* 7 (1974): 9-44.

Stokes, Adrian. *Greek Culture and the Ego: A Psychoanalytic Survey of an Aspect of Greek Civilization and of Art*. London: Tavistock Publications, 1958.

Strunsky, S. "The Scandal of Euclid: A Freudian Analysis." *Atlantic Monthly* 124 (1919): 332-37.

Sunden, Hjalmar. "Die Personlichkeit der Heiligen Birgitta: Versuch einer 'Rollenpsychologischen' Untersuchung." *Archiv für Religions-psychologie* 10 (1971): 249-59.

*Tarachow, Sidney, "St. Paul and Early Christianity." *Psychoanalysis and the Social Sciences* 4, 1955.

Velikovsky, Immanuel. *Oedipus and Akhnaton, Myth and History*. Garden City, N.Y.: Doubleday, 1960.

Vernant, Jean-Pierre. *Mythe et Pensee Chez les Grecs*. Maspero, 1965.

Veszy-Wagner, L. "The Independent Fledgling." *The Psychoanalytic Review* 50, 1963.

Weigert-Vorwinkel, Edith. "The Cult and Mythology of the Magna Mater From the Standpoint of Psychoanalysis." *Psychiatry* 1, 1938.

Weyl, Nathaniel. "Some Possible Genetic Implications of Carthaginian Child Sacrifice." *Perspectives in Biology and Medicine* 12 (1968): 69-78.

Zeligs, Dorothy F. "Abraham and the Covenant of the Pieces. A Study in Ambivalence." *American Imago* 18 (1961): 173-86.
———. "A Character Study of Samuel. In *The Annual Survey of Psychoanalysis*, pp. 409-411. Ed. by J. Frosch. N.Y.: Intern. Univ. Press, 1955.
———. "The Family Romance of Moses: The 'Personal Myth.' " *American Imago* 23 (1966): 110-31.
———. "Moses Encounters the Daemonic Aspect of God." *American Imago* 27 (1970): 379-392.
———. "Moses in Midian: The Burning Bush." *American Imago* 26 (1969): 379-400.
———. "The Personality of Joseph." In *The Annual Survey of Psychoanalysis*, pp. 408-09. Ed. by J. Frosch. NY: Intern. Univ. Press, 1955.
———. *Psychoanalysis and the Bible*. NY: Bloch Publishing Co., 1974.
———. "The Role of the Mother in the Development of Hebraic Monotheism." *The Psychoanalytic Study of Society* I, 1960.
———. "Solomon: Man and Myth." *Psychoanalysis and the Psychoanalytic Review* 48 (1961): 77-103; no. 2 (1961): 91-110.

IV. MEDIEVAL AND RENAISSANCE

Bainton, Roland. "Luther: A Psychiatric Portrait," *Yale Review*, 48 (1959): 405-10.
———. "Psychiatry and History: An Examination of Erikson's *Young Man Luther*," *Religion in Life*, 40 (1971): 450-78
Benton, John. "Clio and Venus; an Historical View of Medieval Love," in *The Meaning of Courtly Love*, Francis X. Newman, ed. Albany, 1968, 19-42.
———. ed. *Self and Society in Medieval France: The Memoirs of Abbot Guibert of Nogent*. NY: Harper & Row, 1970. Intro. also in *Psychoanalytic Review* 57 (1970-1): 361-82.
Blanchard, William. "Medieval Morality and Juvenile Delinquency." *American Imago* 13 (1956): 383-98.
Bonney, F. "Jean Gerson: Un nouveau regard sur l'enfance." *Annales de Demographie Historique* (1973): 137-42.
Byman, Seymour. "Suicide and Alienation: Martyrdom in Tudor England." *The Psychoanalytic Review* 61 (1974): 355-73.

Coleman, Emily R. "Medieval Marriage Characteristics: A Neglected Factor in the History of Medieval Serfdom." In *The Family in History*. Ed. by Theodore K. Rabb and Robert Rotberg. NY: Harper & Row, 1971.

Domhoff, William G. "Two Luthers: The Traditional and the Heretical in Freudian Psychology." *Psychoanalytic Review* 57 (1970): 5-17.

*Eissler, Kurt R. *Leonardo Da Vinci: Psychoanalytic Notes on the Enigma*. NY: International Univ. Press, Inc., 1961.
*Erikson, Erik H. *Young Man Luther: A Study of Psychoanalysis and History*. NY: Norton, 1958, 1962.

Fife, Robert H. *Young Luther*. (Reprint of 1928 ed.) NY: AMS Press, Inc., 1970.
Flugel, J. C. "On the Character and Married Life of Henry VIII," in Bruce Mazlish (ed.), *Psychoanalysis and History*. NY: Grosset & Dunlap, 1971: 124-49.
Freud, Sigmund, "Leonardo da Vinci and a Memory of His Childhood." *Standard Edition* Vol. XI 63-137.
Forbes, Thomas R. *The Midwife and the Witch*. New Haven: Yale Univ. Press, 1966.

Graham, Thomas F. *Medieval Minds: Mental Health in the Middle Ages*. London, 1967.

Halverson, John. "Amour and Eros in the Middle Ages." *The Psychoanalytic Review* 57 (1970).

Kligerman, Charles. "A Psychoanalytic Study of the Confessions of St. Augustine." *Journal of the American Psychoanalytic Association* 6 (1957): 469-84.

Lawrence, W. J. "The Phallus on the Early English Stage." *Psyche & Eros* 2 (1921): 161-65.

Leclercq, Jean. "Modern Psychology and the Interpretation of Medieval Texts." *Spectrum* 48 (1973): 476-90.

Lindbeck, George A. "Erikson's *Young Man Luther:* A Historical and Theological Reappraisal." *Soundings* 56 (1973): 210-27.

Lombillo, Jose R. "The Soldier Saint: A Psychological Analysis of the Conversion of Ignatius de Loyola." *Psychiatric Quarterly* 47 (1973): 386-414.

Lomer, Georg. *Ignatius von Loyola: Vom Erotiker zum Heiligen; eine pathographische Geschichtsstudie.* Leipzig: Barth, 1913.

Markle, Durward J. "Freud, Leonardo and the Lamb." *Psychoanalytic Review* 57 (1971): 285-88.

Medlicott, R. W. "St. Anthony Abbot and the Hazards of Asceticism." *British Journal of Medieval Psychology* 42 (1969): 133-40.

Moller, Herbert. "The Meaning of Courtly Love." *Journal of American Folklore* 73 (1960).

——. "The Social Causation of the Courtly Love Complex," *Comparative Studies in Society and History* 1 (1959).

Muschg, Walter. *Die Mystik in der Schweiz, 1200-1500.* N.p.: Frankenfeld, 1935.

Myer, John C. "Erasmus, Luther, and Machiavelli: A Study of Dissonance." *Psychology* 5 no. 2 (1968): 42-44.

Niederland, William G. "The Naming of America." In Mark Kanzer, ed. *The Unconscious Today.* NY: International Universities Press, 1971.

Peacock, James L. "Mystics and Merchants in Fourteenth Century Germany: A Speculative Reconstruction of their Psychological Bond and Its Implication for Social Change." *Journal for the Scientific Study of Religion* 8 (1969): 47-59.

Petrus, Earl P. "The Golem: Significance of the Legend." *The Psychoanalytic Review* 53 (Spring, 1966): 63-68.

Pfister, Oscar. *Christianity and Fear.* London: Allen and Unwin, 1948.

Pruyser, Paul W. "Erikson's *Young Man Luther:* A New Chapter in the Psychology of Religion." *Journal for the Scientific Study of Religion,* 2 (1962-3): 238-42.

Saffady, William. "Fears of Sexual License During the English Reformation." *History of Childhood Quarterly* 1 (1973): 89-97.

——. "The Effects of Childhood Bereavement and Parental Remarriage in Sixteenth-Century England: The Case of Thomas More." *History of Childhood Quarterly* 1 (1973): 310-336.

Schapiro, Meyer. "Leonardo and Freud: An Art Historical Study." *Journal of the History of Ideas* (April, 1956).

Sereno, Renzo. "A Falsification of Machiavelli," in Bruce Mazlish (ed.), *Psychoanalysis and History.* NY: Grosset & Dunlap, 1971: 108-14.

Shore, Miles F. "Henry VIII and the Crisis of Generativity." *Journal of Interdisciplinary History* 2 (1972): 359-390.

Smith, Preserved. "Luther's Early Development in the Light of Psychoanalysis." *American Journal of Psychology* 24 (1913): 360-377.

Spitz, Lewis W. "Psychohistory and History: The Case of *Young Man Luther.*" *Soundings* 56 (1973): 182-209.

Stites, Raymond S. *The Sublimation of Leonardo da Vinci.* Washington, D.C.: Smithsonian Institution Press, 1970.

Woollcott, Philip. "Creativity and Religious Experience in St. Augustine." *Journal for Scientific Study of Religion* 5 (1966): 273-83.

Zilboorg, Gregory. *The Medical Man and the Witch During the Renaissance.* NY: Cooper Square Publishers, 1969.

V. MODERN

Ackerman, Nathan and Marie Jahoda, *Anti-Semitism and Emotional Disorder: A Psychoanalytic Interpretation*. NY: International Universities Press, 1950.

Adorno, Theodor W. "Anti-Semitism and Fascist Propaganda." In *Anti-Semitism: A Social Disease*. Ed. by Ernst Simmel. NY: Intl. Univ. Press, 1946.

———. "Freudian Theory and the Pattern of Fascist Propaganda." In *Psychoanalysis and the Social Sciences*. Ed. by Geza Roheim. NY: International Univ. Press, 1950, pp. 279-300.

Alexander, A. "War Crimes: Their Socio-Psychological Aspects." *American Journal of Psychiatry* 105 (1948): 170-77.

Alexander, Leo. "Sociopsychologic Structure of the SS: Psychiatric Report of The Nürnberg Trials for War Crimes." *Archives of Neurology and Psychiatry* 59 (1948): 622-34.

———. "War Crimes: Their Social-Psychological Aspects." *The American Journal of Psychiatry* 105 (1948): 170-77.

Alexander, Franz. "Problems of a Wartime Society." *American Journal of Orthopsychiatry* 13 (1943): 571-80.

Allport, Gordon. "Personality Under Social Catastrophe: 90 Life Histories of the Nazi Revolution." *Character and Personality* 10 (1941): 1-22.

Allport, G. W., J. S. Bruner and E. M. Jundorf. "Personality under Social Catastrophe: Ninety Life-Histories of the Nazi Revolution." In Clyde Kluckhohn and Henry Murray, *Personality in Nature, Society and Culture*. NY: Knopf, 1955: 436-55.

Anderson, F. A. "Psychopathological Glimpses of Some Biblical Characters." *Psychoanalytic Review* 14 (1927): 56-70.

Anderson, Michael. "Family, Household and the Industrial Revolution." In *The American Family in Social-Historical Perspective*. Ed. by Michael Gordon. NY: St. Martin's Press, 1974.

Ansbacher, H. L., et al. "Lee Harvey Oswald: An Adlerian Interpretation." *Psychoanalytic Review* 53 (1966): 55-68.

Axtell, James L. "Coming of Age in Colonial America: A New Look." Paper read at the annual convention of the American Historical Association, Dec. 30, 1970 at Boston, Mass.

Barber, James D. "Adult Identity and Presidential Style: The Rhetorical Emphasis," in Dankwart A. Rustow (ed.), *Philosophers and Kings: Studies in Leadership*. NY: George Braziller, 1970: 367-97.

———. "President Nixon & Richard Nixon: Character Trap." *Psychology Today*, 8 (Oct. 1974): 112-21.

*———. *The Presidential Character: Predicting Performance in the White House*. Englewood Cliffs: Prentice-Hall, Inc., 1972;

*Barker-Benfield, Ben. "The Spermatic Economy: A Nineteenth-Century View of Sexuality." In *The American Family in Social-Historical Perspective*. Ed. by Michael Gordon. NY: St. Martin's Press, 1974.

Bartlett, Irving H. and Richard L. Schoenwald. "The Psychodynamics of Slavery." *Journal of Interdisciplinary History* 4 (1974): 627-34.

Battis, Emery J. *Saints and Sectarians: Anne Hutchinson and the Antinomian Controversy in Massachusetts Bay Colony*. Chapel Hill: Univ. of N. Carolina Press, 1962.

Bauer, Raymond A. "The Psycho-Cultural Approach to Soviet Studies." *World Politics* 7 no. 1 (1954): 119-32.

———. "The Psychology of the Soviet Middle Elite: Two Case Histories." In Clyde Kluckhohn and Henry Murray (ed.), *Personality in Nature, Society and Culture*. NY: Knopf (1955): 633-50.

Beckman, A. C. "Hidden Themes in the Frontier Thesis: An Application of Psychoanalysis to Historiography." *Comparative Studies in Society and History* 8 (April, 1966): 361-82.

Bender, Lauretta and Frosch, J. "Children's Reaction to the War." *American Journal of Orthopsychiatry* 12 (1942): 571-87.

Beradt, C. *The Third Reich of Dreams*. NY: Quadrangle Books, 1966.

*Bergler, Edmund. *Talleyrand, Napoleon, Stendahl, Grabbe. Psychoanalytisch-biographische Essays.* Vienna: Internationale Psychoanal. Verlag, 1935.

Bettelheim, Bruno. *The Informed Heart: Autonomy in a Mass Age.* Glencoe, Ill., 1960.

Binger, Carl. "Conflicts in the Life of Thomas Jefferson." *American Journal of Psychiatry* 125 (1969): 1098-107.

———. "The Dreams of Benjamin Rush." *American Journal of Psychiatry* 125 (June 1969): 1653-59.

Binion, Rudolph. "MyLife With Frau Lou." In *The Historians Workshop,* pp. 293-306. Ed. by L. P. Curtis, Jr. NY: 1970.

*———. *Frau Lou: Nietzsche's Wayward Disciple.* Princeton, N.J.: Princeton Univ. Press, 1968.

———. "From Mayerling to Sarajevo," forthcoming in *Journal of Modern History.* June 1975.

*———. "Hitler's Concept of *Lebensraum:* The Psychological Basis." *History of Childhood Quarterly* 1 (1973): 187-215, 249-58.

———. "Repeat Performance: A Psychological Study of Leopold III and Belgian Neutrality." *History and Theory* 8 (1969): 213-59.

Blanchard, Phyllis Mary. "A Psychoanalytic Study of Auguste Comte." *American Journal of Psychology* 29 (1918): 159-181.

*Blanchard, William. *Rousseau and the Spirit of Revolt: A Psychological Study.* Ann Arbor: The Univ. of Michigan Press, 1967.

Bogardus, Emorys. "Albert Schweitzer as a Leader." *Sociology and Social Research* 42 (1957): 46-53.

Bonnard, Augusta. "The Metapsychology of the Russian Trial Confessions." *International Journal of Psycho-Analysis* 35 (1954): 208-13.

Bridenthal, Renate. "Beyond Kinder, Küche, Kirche: Weimar Women at Work," paper read at the annual convention of the American Historical Association, Dec. 28, 1971, at New York, N.Y.

Brodie, Bernard. "A Psychoanalytic Interpretation of Woodrow Wilson." *World Politics* 9 (1957): 413-422. Also in Bruce Mazlish, ed., *Psychoanalysis and History* (NY: Grosset & Dunlap, 1971), pp. 115-23.

Brodie, Fawn M. "Jefferson Biographers and the Psychology of Canonization." *Journal of Interdisciplinary History* II (1971): 155-72.

———. *Thaddeus Stevens: Scourge of the South.* NY: Norton & Co., 1959.

———. *Thomas Jefferson: An Intimate History.* NY: Norton, 1973.

Bromberg, Norbert. "Hitler's Character and Its Development: Further Observations." *American Imago* 28 (1971): 289-303.

———. "Totalitarian Ideology as a Defence Technique." *The Psychoanalytic Study of Society* 1 (1960): 26-38.

———. "The Psychotic Character as Political Leader." Parts I and II. Unpub. papers read at Annual Meetings of the American Psychoanalytic Association 1961, 1962.

Brophy, Briget. *Black Ship to Hell.* NY: Harcourt, Brace, Jovanovich, 1962.

Brown, William. "The Psychology of Modern Germany." *British Journal of Psychology* 34 (1944): 43-59.

Bullough, Vern L. "Exploring a Virgin Field: Sex in European History," paper read at the annual convention of the American Historical Association, Dec. 29, 1970 at Boston, Mass.

Bushman, Richard L. *From Puritan to Yankee: Character and the Social Order in Connecticut, 1690-1765.* Cambridge: Harvard Univ. Press, 1967.

———. "Jonathan Edwards as Great Man: Identity Conversion, and Leadership in the Great Awakening." *Soundings* 52 (1969): 15-46.

———. "Jonathan Edwards and Puritan Consciousness." *Journal of the Scientific Study of Religion* 5 (1966): 383-96.

Burnham, John C. "The Place of Sex in the Study of American History," paper read at the annual convention of the American Historical Association, Dec. 29, 1970, at Boston, Mass.

Bychowsky, Gustav. "Joseph Stalin: Paranoia and the Dictatorship of the Proletariat." In *The Psychoanalytic Interpretation of History.* Ed. by B. R. Wolman. NY: Basic Books, 1971: 115-49.

———. "Oliver Cromwell and the Puritan Revolution." *Journal of Clinical Psycho-*

pathology 7 (1945): 281-309.

———. "The Potential of Psychoanalytic Biography: Zeligs on Chambers and Hiss." *American Imago* 26 (1969): 233-41.

———. "Robespierre and the Terror." *Journal of Clinical Psychopathology* 7 (1945-46): 561-98.

———. "The Spiritual Background of Hitlerism." *Journal of Clinical Psychopathology* 4 (1943): 579-98.

Calhoun, Daniel. *The Intelligence of a People.* Princeton: Princeton University Press, 1973.

Capps, Donald. "John Henry Newman: A Study of Vocational Identity." *Journal for the Scientific Study of Religion* 9 (1970): 33-52.

———. "Orestes Brownson: The Psychology of Religious Affiliation." *Journal for the Study of Religion* 7 (1968): 197-209.

———. "The 'Reversal of Generations' Phenomenon as Illustrated by the Lives of John Henry Newman and Abraham Lincoln," paper read at the annual convention of the American Historical Association, Dec. 29, 1973 at San Francisco, Calif.

Chamberlain, Frederick. *The Private Character of Queen Elizabeth.* London: Bodley Head, 1921.

Chanover, E. Pierre. "Jean-Jacques Rousseau: A Psychoanalytic and Psychological Bibliography." *American Imago* 31 (1974): 95-100.

Chesen, Eli S. *President Nixon's Psychiatric Profile.* NY: Peter H. Wyden, 1973.

Clark, L. Pierce. *Lincoln: A Psycho-Biography.* NY: Scribner, 1933.

———. "Unconscious Motives Underlying the Personalities of Great Statesmen and Their Relation to Epoch-Making Events: A Psychoanalytic Study of Abraham Lincoln." *Psychoanalytic Review* 8 (1921): 1-21. Also in *Psychological Studies of Famous Americans.* Ed. by Norman Kiell. NY: Twayne Publishers, Inc., 1964.

Cohen, Elie A. *Human Behavior in the Concentration Camp.* NY: Norton, 1953.

Cominos, Peter T. "Innocent Femina Sensualis in Unconscious Conflict," in Martha Vicinus, ed., *Suffer and Be Still: Women in the Victorian Age.* Bloomington: Indiana Univ. Press, 1972: 155-72.

———. "Late-Victorian Sexual Respectability and the Social System." *International Review of Social History* 8 (1963): 18-48; 216-50.

Confino, Michaël. "Histoire et psychologie: A propos de la noblesse russe qu XVIIᵉ siècle," *Annales: économies, sociétés, civilisations* 22 (1967): 1163-205.

Clinch, Nancy G. *The Kennedy Neurosis.* NY: Grosset & Dunlap, 1973.

Daberman, Martin B. "The Abolitionists and Psychology." *Journal of Negro History* 47 (1962): 183-91.

Dadrian, Vabraken N. "Factors of Anger and Aggression in Genocide." *Journal of Human Relations* 19 no. 3 (1971): 394-417.

Davis, David Brion. *The Slave Power Conspiracy and the Paranoid Style.* Baton Rouge: LSU Press, 1969.

———. "Some Themes of Countersubversion: An Analysis of Anti-Masonic, Anti-Catholic, and Anti-Mormon Literature." *The Mississippi Valley Historical Review* 47 (1960): 205-24.

Davis, Glenn. "The Early Years of Theodore Roosevelt: A Study in Character Formation." *The History of Childhood Quarterly* 2 (1975): 461-492.

de Certeau, Michel. "Ce que Freud fait de l'histoire: A Propos du 'Une nervose demoniaque au XVIIᵉ siecle'," *Annales: Economies, Societes, Civilisations* 25 (1970): 654-67.

Demole, V. "Analyse Psychiatrique des Confessions de Jean-Jacques Rousseau." *Schweizer Archiv für Neurologie und Psychiatrie* 2 (1918): 270-304.

———. "Role du Tempérament et des Idées Délirantes de Rousseau Dans la Genèse de ses Principales Théories." *Annales Medico-Psychologiques* 12 no. 1 (1922): 12-34.

Demos, John. "The American Puritan as a Psychological Type," paper read at the annual convention of the American Historical Association, Dec. 28, 1972, at New Orleans, La.

———. "Underlying Themes in the Witchcraft of Seventeenth-Century New Eng-

land." *American Historical Review* LXXV (1970): 1311-326.
Desmonde, William H. "The Ku Klux Klan: Some Psychoanalytic Interpreta-tions." *Journal of the Hillside Hospital* 3 (1954): 219-25.
Devoto, Andrea. "Il Languaggio del 'Lager': Annotazione Psychologiche." *Movimento di Liberazione in Italia* 65 no. 4 (1961): 32-48.
Dew, C. B. "Two Approaches to Southern History: Psychology and Quantifica-tion." *South Atlantic Quarterly* 66 (1967): 307-25.
*Dicks, Henry V. *Licensed Mass Murder: A Socio-Psychological Study of Some S.S. Killers.* NY: Basic Books, Inc., 1972.
——. "Observations on Contemporary Russian Behavior." *Human Relations* 5 (1952): 111-77.
——. "Personality Traits and National Socialistic Ideology." *Human Relations* 3 (1950): 111-54.
——. Psychological Studies of the German Character", in T. Pear, ed., *Psychological Factors of Peace and War.* NY: Philosophical Library, 1951.
Dittmar, L. "A Psycho-Sociological Analysis of Neo-Naziism." *Comparative Politics* 2 (1969).
Dubbert, Joe L. "Progressivism and the Masculinity Crisis." *The Psychoanalytic Review* 61 (1974): 443-55.
Duff, I. F. Grant. "Die Beziehung Elizabeth-Essex: eine psychoanalytische Be-trachtung." *Psychoanalytische Bewehgung* 3 (1931): 457-74.
Dufreniy, M. L. "La Psychopathologie de Jean-Jacques Rousseau." *Revue de Pathologie Comparée et de Médicine Expérimentale,* Paris 67 (1967): 245-54.
Dunn, Patrick P. "Fathers and Sons Revisited: The Childhood of Vissarion Belin-skii." *History of Childhood Quarterly* 1 (1974): 389-409.
Durkham, John. "The Influence of John Stuart Mill's Mental Crisis on his Thoughts." *American Imago* 20 (1963): 369-84.

Ebel, Henry. "Primal Therapy and Psychohistory." *History of Childhood Quarterly* 2 (1975): 563-570
Edinger, Lewis J. *Kurt Schumacher: A Study in Personality and Political Behavior.* Stanford, Cal.: Stanford Univ. Press, 1965.
Edwards, Maldwyn. *Family Circle: A Study in the Epworth Household in Rela-tion to John and Charles Wesley.* London: The Epworth Press, 1949.
Elkins, Stanley. *Slavery.* Chicago: Univ. of Chicago Press, 1959.
Erikson, Erik H. "Hitler's Imagery and German Youth." *American Psychiatry Journal* 5 (1942): 475-93. Also in *Personality in Nature, Society and Culture,* pp. 485-510. Ed. by C. Kluckholm and H. A. Murray. NY: Knopf, 1948.
——. "Wholeness and Totality—A Psychiatric Contribution." In *Totalitarianism.* Ed. by Earl J. Friedrich. Cambridge: Harvard Univ. Press, 1954.
Evans, W. N. "The Passing of the Gentleman." *Psychoanalytic Quarterly* 18 (1949): 19-43.

Feinstein, Howard. "Benjamin Rush: A Child of Light for the Children of Dark-ness." *Psychoanalytic Review* 58 (1971): 209-22.
——. "The Prepared Heart: Puritan Theology and Psychoanalysis." *American Quarterly* 22 (1970): 166-76.
Feldman, A. Bronson. "Ben Franklin—Thunder Master." *Psychoanalysis* 5 (1957): 33-54.
——. "The Imperial Dreams of Disraeli." *Psychoanalytic Review* 53 no. 4 (1966): 109-41.
——. "Lincoln: the Psychology of a Cult." *Journal of the National Psychological Association for Psychoanalysis* 1 (1952): 7-24. Also in *Psychological Studies of Famous Americans,* pp. 116-34. Ed. by Norman Kiell. NY: Twayne Publishers, Inc., 1964.
Fenichel, Otto. "Psychoanalysis of Antisemitism." *American Imago* 1 (1940): 24-39.
Ferdon, Nona Stinson. "Franklin D. Roosevelt: A Psychological Interpretation of his Childhood and Youth." Unpublished doctoral dissertation, Univ. of Hawaii, 1971.
Feuer, Lewis S. *Conflict of Generations: Character and Significance of Student Movements.* NY: Basic Books, 1969.

———. "Ernst Mach: The Unconscious Motives of an Empiricist." *American Imago* 27 (1970): 12-39.

Filene, Peter G. "Men and Manliness Before World War I–A Study in Changing Male Sex Roles," paper read at the annual convention of the Organization of American Historians, April 7, 1972, at Washington, D.C.

Fitzpatrick, John J. "Senator Hiram W. Johnson: A Life History, 1866-1945," unpublished doctoral dissertation, Univ of Calif, Berkeley, 1975.

Flugel, John Carl. *Man, Morals and Society: A Psycho-Analytical Study.* NY: International Univ. Press, 1945.

———. *Psychoanalytic Study of the Family.* NY: Hillary House, n.d.

Foucault, Michael. *Madness and Civilization: A History of Insanity in the Age of Reason.* NY: Pantheon Books, 1965.

Fox, Ezra G. Benedict. "Was General Lee a Victim of Group Psychology?" In *Psychological Studies of Famous Americans.* Ed. by Norman Kiell. NY: Twayne Publishers, Inc., 1964.

Franzoni, Janet Brenner. "The Private War of General Sherman," unpublished MA thesis, University of N. Carolina, Greensboro, 1970.

———. "Troubled Tirader: A Psychological Study of Tom Watson." *Georgia Historical Quarterly* 57 (1973): 493-510.

Freud, Sigmund. "A Seventeenth-Century Demonological Neurosis." *Standard Edition* Vol. XIX: 72-108.

——— and William C. Bullett. *Thomas Woodrow Wilson: A Psychological Study.* Boston: Houghton Mifflin, 1967.

Frijling-Schreuder, E. C. M. "Honore de Balzac: A Disturbed Boy Who Did Not Get Treatment." *Intern'l Journal of Psycho-Analysis* 45 (1964): 426-30.

Fromm, Erich. "On the Problems of German Characterology." *Transactions of the New York Academy of Sciences* 5 (1943): 79-83.

———. "Should We Hate Hitler?" *Journal of Home Economics* 34 (1942): 220-23.

———. "What Shall We do With Germany?" *Sat. Rev. of Lit.,* May 29, 1943.

Gardner, George E. "The Family in a World at War." *Mental Hygiene* 26 (1942): 50-7.

Gatell, Frank Otto. "The Social and Psychological Dynamics of Change: From the Bank to Slavery," paper read at the annual convention of the American Historical Association, Dec. 29, 1969, at Washington, D.C.

Gatzke, Hans W. "Hitler and Psychohistory." *American Historical Review* 78 (April, 1973): 394-401.

George, Alexander L. "Assessing Presidential Character." *World Politics* 26 (1974): 234-82.

——— and George, Juliett L. *Woodrow Wilson and Colonel House: A Personality Study.* NY: Day, 1956.

Gilbert, G. M. "Goering, Amiable Psychopath." *Journal of Abnormal and Social Psychology* 43 (1948): 211-29.

———. *Nuremberg Diary.* NY: Farrar, Strauss, and Co., 1947.

*———. *The Psychology of Dictatorship.* NY: The Roland Press, 1950.

Gilmore, William J. "The Nature and Context of Reform in America 1815-1835, and the Generation of 1830," paper read at the annual convention of the American Historical Association, Dec. 29, 1970, at Boston, Mass.

———. "The Problems and Dangers of 'Originitis' in Psycho-History: The Early Years of Orestes Brownson," paper read at the annual convention of the Organization of American Historians, April 13, 1973, at Chicago, Ill.

———. " 'A Volcano with an Ordinary Chimney-Flue'; The Development of John Brown's Personality," paper read at the annual convention of the Organization of American Historians, April 1974 at Denver, Colo.

Glad, Betty. *Charles Evans Hughes and the Illusions of Innocence.* Urbana: Univ. of Illinois Press, 1966.

———. "The Significance of Personality for Role Performance as Chairman of the Senate Foreign Relations Committee: A Comparison of Borah and Fulbright," unpub. paper read at the American Political Science Assoc. meeting, 1969.

Glover, Edward. *War, Sadism and Pacifism.* London: Allen & Unwin, 1935, 1946.

Gonen, Jay Y. *A Psychohistory of Zionism.* NY: Mason&Carter Publishers, 1974.

Gorer, Geoffrey. *The American People: A Study in National Character.* NY: Norton, 1948.

——. *Exploring English Character.* NY: 1955.

——. *The People of Great Russia.* NY: Chanticleer, 1950.

Gottfried, Alex. *Boss Cermak of Chicago. A Study of Political Leadership.* Seattle, 1962: 365-78. Also appears as "The Use of Psychosomatic Categories in a Study of Political Personality." *Western Political Quarterly* 8 (1955): 234-47.

Greenacre, Phyllis. *Swift and Carroll: A Psychological Study of Two Lives.* NY: 1955.

Greenblatt, Robert B. "Hermann Goering's Pseudo-Fröhlich Syndrome." *Medical Aspects of Human Sexuality* 6 (1972): 94-104.

Greene, Jack P. "Search for Identity: An Interpretation of the Meaning of Selected Patterns of Social Response in Eighteenth Century America." *Journal of Social History* 3 (1970): 189-220.

Greven, Philip J., Jr. "The Child and the Convert: Reflections on Jonathan Edwards and the Psychology of Religious Experience in Eighteenth Century America," paper read at the annual convention of the American Historical Association, Dec. 28, 1970 at Boston, Mass.

——. *Four Generations: Population, Land and Family in Colonial Andover, Mass.* Ithaca, N.Y.: Cornell Univ. Press, 1970.

Hale, William Bayard. *The Story of Style. A Psychoanalytic Study of Woodrow Wilson.* NY: Viking Press, 1920.

Haque, John. *American Character and Culture.* DeLand: Florida: Everett-Edwards, 1964.

Hargrove, Erwin. *Presidential Leadership: Personality and Political Leadership.* NY: Macmillan, 1966.

Harlow, Ralph. "A Psychological Study of Samuel Adams." *Psychoanalytic Review* 9 (1922): 418-28.

——. *Samuel Adams, Promoter of the American Revolution: A Study in Psychology and Politics.* NY: H. Holt & Co., 1923.

Harris, Ramon I. "Thomas Jefferson: Female Identification." *American Imago* 25 (1968): 371-83.

Hartman, D. A. "The Psychological Point of View in History: Some Phases of the Slavery Struggle." In *Psychological Studies of Famous Americans.* Ed. by Norman Kiell. NY: Twayne, 1964.

Hawke, David. *Paine.* NY: Harper & Row, 1974.

Hector, L. S. "An Alleged Hysterical Outburst of Richard II." *English Historical Review* 68 (1953): 62-5.

Henretta, J. "The Morphology of New England Society in the Colonial Period." In *The Family in History.* NY: Harper & Row, 1971.

Herman, I. "Charles Darwin." *Imago* 13 (1927): 57-82.

Hesseltine, William B. "Forty Years of Failure." [Ulysses S. Grant.] In *Psychological Studies of Famous Americans.* Ed. by Normal Kiell. NY: Twayne, 1964.

Hitschmann, Edward. "Boswell: The Biographer's Character: A Psychoanalytic Interpretation." *Psychoanalytic Quarterly* 17 (1948): 212-25

Hoffman, Stanley. "Vichy's Main Actors: Social and Psychological Dimensions," paper read at the annual convention of the American Historical Association, Dec. 29, 1969, at Washington, D.C.

Hofling, Charles K. "General Custer and the Battle of the Little Big Horn." *Psychoanalytic Review* 54 (1967): 107-32.

Hofstadter, Richard. "The Paranoid Style in American Politics." In Hofstadter, *The Paranoid Style in American Politics and Other Essays.* NY: Knopf, 1964, 1965.

Hogeland, Ronald W. "The Concept of the American Woman: Horace Bushnell, A Case Study in Masculine Ambivalence," paper read at the annual convention of the American Historical Association, Dec. 30, 1969, at Washington, D.C.

Homans, Peter. "Transcendence, Distance, Fantasy: The Protestant Era in Psychological Perspective." *Journal of Religion,* 49 (1969): 205-27.

Hoppe, Klaus et al., "The Emotional Reactions of Psychiatrists When Confronting Survivors of Persecution." *The Psychoanalytic Forum* 3 (1969): 185-211.

Hoppe, Klaus D. "The Psychodynamics of Concentration Camp Victims." *The*

Psychoanalytic Forum 1 (1966): 76-80. NY: International Univ. Press.
Hunt, Richard MacMasters. "Joseph Goebbels." Ph.D. Dissertation, Harvard Univ., 1960.
Hunter, Doris M. and Charlotte Babcock. "Some Aspects of the Intrapsychic Structure of Certain American Negroes as Viewed in the Intercultural Dynamic," in Wilbur Muensterberger, ed., *The Psychoanalytic Study of Society.* NY: 1967: 124-169.

Inkeles, Alex. "National Character and Modern Political Systems." In *Psychological Anthropology,* pp. 172-208. Ed. by F. Hsu. Homewood: Dorsey Press, 1961.
—— and David H. Smith. "The Fate of Personal Adjustment in the Process of Modernization." *International Journal of Comparative Sociology* 11 (1970): 81-114.
Izenberg, Gerald N. "The Wish to Be Free." *Journal of Interdisciplinary History* 2 (1971): 137-48.

Janis, Irving L. *Victims of Groupthink: A Psychological Study of Foreign-Policy Decisions and Fiascoes.* Boston: Houghton Mifflin, 1972.
*Jardim, Anne. *The First Henry Ford: A Study in Personality and Business Leadership.* Cambridge: The MIT Press, 1970.
Jekels, Ludwig. *Selected Papers.* NY: International Univ. Press, 1970.
——. "The Turning Point in the Life of Napoleon I." In his *Selected Papers.* NY: International Univ. Press, 1970.
Jones, Ernest. "The Case of Louis Bonaparte, King of Holland." In *Essays in Applied Psycho-Analysis.* London: The Hogarth Press, 1951.
——. "The Inferiority Complex of the Welsh." *Welsh Outlook* 16 (1929): 76-77.
——. "The Island of Ireland. A Psycho-Analytical Contribution to Political Psychology." In *Essays in Applied Psycho-Analysis,* pp. 95-112. London: The Hogarth Press, 1951.
Jordon, Winthrop. "Familial Politics: Thomas Paine and the Killing of the King, 1776." *Journal of American History* 60 (1973): 294-308.
Jowitt, Th. Earl. *The Strange Case of Alger Hiss.* Garden City, N.Y., 1953.
Jung, E. "Jean-Jacques Rousseau also Psychoanalytiker." *Internationale Zeitschrift für Psychoanalyse* 3 (1912-1913): 52.

Kakar, Sudhir. *Frederick Taylor: A Study in Personality and Innovation.* Cambridge, Mass.: 1970.
Kardiner, Abraham and Lionel Ovesey. *The Mark of Oppression: Explorations in the Personality of the American Negro.* Cleveland: World, 1967.
Katz, Joseph. "President Kennedy's Assassination." *The Psychoanalytic Review* 51 no. 4 (1964-65): 121-24.
Kedro, Milan James. "Autobiography as a Key to Identity in the Progressive Era." *History of Childhood Quarterly* 2 (1975): 391-407.
Keller, Phyllis. "George Sylvester Viereck: the Psychology of a German-American Militant." *Journal of Interdisciplinary History* 2 (1971): 59-108.
Kempf, Edward J. *Abraham Lincoln's Philosophy of Common Sense: An Analytical Biography of a Great Mind.* NY: N.Y. Academy of Sciences, 1965.
——. "Abraham Lincoln's Organic and Emotional Neurosis." *The Psychoanalytic Quarterly* 22 (1953): 306. Also in *Psychological Studies of Famous Americans.* Ed. by Norman Kiell. NY: Twayne, 1964.
——. "Charles Darwin: The Affective Sources of his Inspiration and Anxiety Neurosis." *Psychoanalytic Review* 5 (1918): 151-92.
Kennedy, David M. "Sexual Roles in the Late Nineteenth Century." Paper read at the annual convention of the Organization of American Historians, April 18, 1970, at Los Angeles, Calif.
Kiell, Norman, ed. *Psychological Studies of Famous Americans: The Civil War Era.* NY: Twayne, 1964.
Klaf, Franklin S. "Napoleon and the Grand Army of 1812: A Study of Group Psychology." *Psychoanalysis and the Psychoanalytic Rev.* 47 (1960: 67-76.
Kligerman, Charles. "The Character of Jean Jacques Rousseau." In *The Annual*

Survey of Psychoanalysis 2 (1951): 464-65.

Koenigsberg, Richard A. "Culture and Unconscious Phantasy: Observations on Nazi Germany." *Psychoanalytic Review* 55 (1968-1969): 681-96.

König-Fachsenfeld, O. F. Von. *Wandlungen des Traumproblems von der Romantik bis zur Gegenwart.* Stuttgart: Enke, 1935.

Kovel, Joel. *White Racism: A Psychohistory.* Pantheon, 1970.

Kren, George M. "Race and Ideology." *Phylon,* 23 (1962): 167-77.

—— and Leon Rappoport. "Victims: The Fallacy of Innocence." *Societas—A Review of Social History* 4 (1974): 111-29.

Krystal, Henry, ed. *Massive Psychic Trauma.* NY: 1968.

Künzli, Arnold. *Karl Marx. Eine Psychographie.* Wien, Frankfurt, Zürich, 1966.

Kurth, Gertrude M. "The Jew and Adolph Hitler." *Psychoanalytic Quarterly* 16 (1947): 11-32.

LaBarre, Weston. *They Shall Take Up Serpents: Psychology of the Southern Snake-Handling Cult.* NY: Schocken, 1962, 1969.

——. "Hitler's Imagery and German Youth." *Psychiatry* 5 (1942): 475-93.

Lacombe, Pierre. "The Enigma of Clemenceau." *Psychoanalytic Quarterly* 33 (1946): 165-76.

Laforge, R. "Etude sur Jean-Jacques Rousseau." *Revue Francaise de Psychoanalyse* 1 (1927): 370-402. And in *Psychopathologie de l'Echec,* pp. 117-44. Geneve: Les Editions du Mont-Blanc, 1963.

——. "Jean-Jacques Rousseau. Eine psychoanalytische untersuchung." *Imago* 16 (1930: 145-72.

Lane, Ann, ed. *The Debate Over Slavery: Stanley Elkins and His Critics.* Urbana: Univ. of Illinois Press, 1971.

Langer, Walter C. *The Mind of Adolf Hitler.* NY: Basic Books, 1972.

——; Kris, Ernst and Lewin, Bertram D. *A Psychological Analysis of Adolph Hitler.* Washington: Office of Strategic Services, 1944.

Latif, Israil. "A Psychoanalytic Study of Adolf Hitler." *Journal of Psychoanalysis, Pakistan,* 1 (1953): 25-32

Lawrence, W. J. "The Singing Eunuch in Seventeenth Century England." *Psyche and Eros* 2 (1921): 370-74.

Lawrence, Margaret. *Young Inner City Families: Identity and Development of Ego Strengths.* NY: Behavioral Publications, Inc., 1974.

Leites, Nathan. "Panic and Defenses Against Panic in the Bolshevik View of Politics." *Psychoanalysis and the Social Sciences* 4, 1955.

——. *A Study of Bolshevism.* Glencoe, Ill: The Free Press, 1953.

—— and Paul Kecskemeti. "Some Psychological Hypotheses on Nazi Germany." *Journal of Social Psychology* 26 (1947): 141-83; 27 (1948): 91-117, 241-70; 28 (1948): 141-64.

Leonard, Thomas C. "The Army Officer and the Indian: Psychological Ambivalence and Cultural Relativism," paper read at the annual convention of the American Historical Assoc., Dec. 29, 1973, at San Francisco, Calif.

Levi, A. W. "The 'Mental Crisis' of John Stuart Mill." *Psychoanalytic Review* 32 (1945): 86-101.

Levinson, Daniel J. "Personality and Foreign Policy." *Journal of Conflict of Resolution* (1957): 37-47.

Levy, David Mordecai. "Anti-Nazis: Criteria of Differentiation." *International Journal of Psycho-Analysis* 11 (1948): 125-67.

——. "The German Anti-Nazi: A Case Study." *American Journal of Orthopsychiatry* 16 (1946): 507-515.

Lewin, Kurt. "Some Social-Psychological Differences Between the U.S. and Germany." *Character and Personality* 4 (1936): 265-93.

Lewy, Ernst. "The Transformation of Frederic the Great." In *The Psychoanalytic Study of Society* 4: 252-311.

Liebert, Robert S. "Radical and Militant Youth: A Study of Columbia Undergraduates." In *The Psychoanalytic Forum v. 4,* pp. 1-62. NY: International Univ. Press, 1972.

Lifton, Robert J. *Death in Life: Survivors of Hiroshima.* NY: Random House, 1967.

Loewenberg, Peter. "The Psychohistorical Origins of the Nazi Youth Cohort." *American Historical Review* 76 (1971): 1457-502.

—— "Psychohistorical Perspectives on Modern German History." Forthcoming

in *Journal of Modern History*. June 1975.
——. "The Psychology of Racism." In Gary B. Nash and Richard Weiss, eds., *The Great Fear*. NY: Holt, Rinehart and Winston, 1970: 186-201.
——. "Model Personality and Psychoanalysis: The German Case," paper read at ann. conv. of Am. Hist. Assoc., Dec. 28, 1972, at New Orleans, La.
——. "Theodore Herzl: A Psychoanalytic Study in Charismatic Political Leadership." In *The Psychoanalytic Interpretation of History*. Ed. by B. R. Wolman. NY: Basic Books, 1971: 150-91.
——. "The Unsuccessful Adolescence of Heinrich Himmler." *American Historical Review* 76 (1971): 612-41.
——. "Walter Rathenau as a Culture Critic," paper read at the annual convention of the American Historical Association, Dec. 30, 1971, at New York, N.Y.
——. "Walter Ratenau and German Society," unpublished doctoral dissertation. Univ. of California, Berkeley, 1966.
Löwenthal, John. "Zur Hakenkreuz-Symbolik." *Zeitschrift für Sexualwissenschaft* 17 (1930: 44-50.
——. "Zum Rathenau-Problem." *Zeitschrift für Sexualwissenschaft* 15 (1928): 369-78.
Loewenstein, Rudolph M. *Christians and Jews: A Psychoanalytic Study*. NY: International Universities Press, 1951.

Macalpine, Ida and Hunter, R. A. "George III's Illness and Its Impact on Psychiatry." *Proceedings of the Royal Society of Medicine* 61 (1968): 1017-26.
——. "The 'Insanity' of King George III: A Classic Case of Porphyria." *British Medical Journal* 1 (1966): 65-71.
—— and Rimington, C. "Porphyria in the Royal Houses of Stuart, Hanover, and Prussia. A Follow-up Study of George III's Illness." *British Medical Journal* 1 (1969): 7-18.
McClelland, David C. "Love and Power: The Psychological Signals of War." *Psychology Today* (Jan. 1975): 44-48.
Macfarlane, Alan. *The Family Life of Ralph Josselin, a Seventeenth Century Clergyman*. Cambridge: Cambridge Univ. Press, 1970.
McGovern, James R. "David Graham Phillips and the Virility Impulse of Progressives." *New England Quarterly* 39 (1966): 334-55.
McGranahan, D. "A Comparison of Social Attitudes Among German and American Youth." *Journal of Abnormal and Social Psychology* 41 (1946).
Mack, John E. "T. E. Lawrence: A Study of Heroism and Conflict." *American Journal of Psychiatry* 125 (1969): 1083-92.
McLean, Helen. "Psychodynamic Factors in Race Relations." *Annals of the American Academy of Political and Social Science*. 254 (1946): 159-66.
Malkin, Edward. "Reich and Rousseau: An Essay in Psycho-history." *American Journal of Psychoanalysis* 34 (1974): 63-80.
Mandrou, Robert. *Introduction à la France moderne [1500-1640]. Essai de psychologie historique*. Paris. 1961.
Mannoni, Dominique. *Prospero and Caliban: The Psychology of Colonization*. NY: Praeger, 1964.
Manuel, Frank E. "Newton as Autocrat of Science," in Dankwart A. Rustow, ed., *Philosophers and Kings: Studies in Leadership*. NY: Braziller, 1970: 398-430.
——. *A Portrait of Isaac Newton*. Cambridge: Harvard Univ. Press, 1968.
*Marvick, Elizabeth W. "Childhood History and Decisions of State: The Case of Louis XIII." *History of Childhood Quarterly* 2 (1974): 135-200.
——. "The Character of Louis XIII: The Role of His Physician." *Journal of Interdisciplinary History* 4 (1974): 347-74.
Mazlish, Bruce. *In Search of Nixon: A Psychohistorical Inquiry*. NY: Basic Books, 1972.
*——. *James and John Stuart Mill: Father and Son in the Nineteenth Century*. NY: Basic Books, 1975.
——. "James Mill and the Utilitarians." *Daedalus,* Summer, 1968.
——. "The Mills: Father and Son." *Horizon* 12 no. 3, Summer, 1970.
——. "Psychohistory and Richard M. Nixon." *Psychology Today* 6 (1972): 77-80.
Mayer, Arno J. "Internal Causes and Purposes of War in Europe 1870-1956: A Research Assignment." *Journal of Modern History* 41 (1969): 291-303.
Meerloo, Jose Abraham Maurits. "The Crime of Menticide." *American Journal of Psychiatry* 107 (1951).

——. *Delusion and Mass-Delusion*. NY: Nervous and Mental Disease Monographs, 1949.
——. "Democracy and Fascism Within Us." In *Total War and the Human Mind*. NY: International Univ. Press, 1945.
——. "Mental Infection and the Swastika." *American Practitioner* 11 (1960).
——. "The Psychology of Treason and Loyalty." *American Journal of Psychotherapy* 8 (1954).
——. *The Rape of the Mind*. NY: Grosset & Dunlap, 1956.
——. "Thought Control and Confession Compulsion." In *Explorations in Psychoanalysis*. NY: Julian Press, 1953.
Menninger, Karl A. "Leopold-Loeb: Mental Hygiene Aspects." *Quarterly Bulletin of the Kansas State Board of Health* 2 (1924): 48-51.
——. "A Psychiatrist Looks at Custer." *Surg. Gynecol. Ob.* 84 (1947): 1008-12.
Mersey. "La Tanatophilie dans la Famille des Habsburg." *Zentralblatt für Psychoanalyse und Psychotherapie* 3 (1913): 627-28.
Middlemore, Merell P. "The Treatment of Bewitchment in a Puritan Community." *International Journal of Psycho-Analysis* 15 (1934): 41-58.
Mitscherlich, Alexander. *Doctors of Infamy. The Story of the Nazi Medical Crimes*. NY: Henry Schuman, 1949.
——. "Jugend in der technischen Welt." *Neue Deutsche Hefte* 4 (1957-58): 396-405.
——. *Society Without the Father*. London: Tavistock, 1969.
Mitzman, Arthur. "Anarchists, Bohemians and Psychoanalysis," paper read at the annual convention of the American Historical Assoc., Dec. 30, 1971, at New York, N.Y.
——. *The Iron Cage: An Historical Interpretation of Max Weber*. NY: Knopf, 1969.
Monaco, Paul. "The Popular Cinema as Reflection of the Group Process in France, 1919-1929." *History of Childhood Quarterly* 1 (1974): 607-36.
Money-Kyrle, Roger A. "Some Aspects of State and Character in Germany." *The Annual Survey of Psychoanalysis* 2 (1951): 510-11.
Moore, Robert L. "Justification Without Joy: Psychohistorical Reflections on John Wesley's Childhood and Conversion." *History of Childhood* 2 (1974): 31-52.
Moulton, Ruth and Alexandra Symonds. "Psychoanalytic Reflections on Woman's Liberation." *Contemporary Psychoanalysis* 8 (1972): 197-228.
Muncy, Raymond Lee. *Sex and Marriage in Utopian Communities: 19th Century America*. Bloomington: Indiana Univ. Press, 1973.
Musto, David F. "The Youth of John Quincy Adams." *Proceedings of the American Philosophical Society* 113 (1969): 269-82.
Myer, John C. "The Romantic Response." *Psychology* 6 no. 2 (1969): 40-47. Examines the Romantic Movement (1750-1850).

Niederland, W. G. "An Analytic Inquiry Into the Life and Work of Heinrich Schliemann." In *Drives, Affects, Behavior*, vo. 2. Ed. by M. Schur. NY: International Univ. Press, n.d.
——. "The History and Meaning of California: A Psychoanalytic Inquiry." *Psychoanalytic Quarterly* 40 (1973): 385-90.

Oppeln-Bronikowski, Friedrich. "Eros als Schicksal bei Friedrich dem Grossen und bei Stendahl. Ein sexualpsychologischer Vergleich." *Psychoanalytische Bewegung* 2 (1930): 314-25.

Parker, Harold T. "The Formation of Napoleon's Personality: An Exploratory Essay." *French Historical Studies* 7 (1971): 6-26.
Perry, Lewis C. "The Neurosis of an Antebellum Reformer: Henry Clarke Wright," paper read at the annual convention of the Organization of American Historians, April 1974, at Denver, Colo.
Pflanze, Otto. "Toward a Psychoanalytic Interpretation of Bismarck." *The American Historical Review* 77 (1972): 419-44.
Potter, David M. *People of Plenty: Economic Abundance and the American Character*. Chicago: Univ. of Chicago Press, 1954.
Playne, Aroline E. *The Neurosis of the Nations*. London: G. Allen & Unwin, 1925.
Prätorius, Numa. "Das Licbesleben Ludwigs XIII von Frankreich." *Abhandlungen*

aus dem Gebeite der Sexual forschung 2 no. 6, 1925.
Prince, Morton. "[Theodore] Roosevelt as Analyzed by the New Psychology."
   New York Times, March 24, 1912, Part 6, pp. 1-2. Also under the title "A
   Scientific Vivisection of Mr. Roosevelt." *Current Literature* 52 (1912): 518-22.
———. *The Psychology of the Kaiser: A Study of His Sentiments and His Ob-
   session.* Boston: Badger, 1915.
Progoff, Ira. "The Psychology of Lee Harvey Oswald: A Jungian Approach."
   Journal of Individual Psychology 23 (1966): 37-47.
Pruyser, Paul W. "Erikson's *Young Man Luther:* A New Chapter in the Psychology
   of Religion." *Journal for the Scientific Study of Religion* 2 (1962-3): 238-42.
Putney, Snell and Gail. *The Adjusted American: Normal Neuroses in the Individual
   and Society.* NY: Norton, 1964.

Raeff, Marc. "Home, School, and Service in the Life of the Eighteenth-Century
   Russian Nobleman." *Slavonic and East European Review* XL, 95 (1962):
   295-307.
Reich, Wilhelm. *The Mass Psychology of Fascism.* NY: Farrar, Straus, 1970.
Reiff, Philip. "Fourteen Points on Wilson." *Encounter* 28 (1967): 85.
Reiners, Ludwig. *The Lamps Went out in Europe.* NY: Pantheon, 1955.
Renshon, Stanley Allen. "Psychological Analysis and Presidential Personality: The
   Case of Richard Nixon." *History of Childhood Quarterly* 2 (1975): 415-50.
Richardson, Frank. *Napoleon: Bisexual Emperor.* NY: Horizon Press, 1973.
Riesman, David. *The Lonely Crowd: A Study of the Changing American Charac-
   ter.* New Haven: Yale Univ. Press, 1950, 1953.
Rinaldo, Joel. *Psychoanalysis of the "Reformer."* NY: Lee Publ. Co., 1921).
Robertson, Paul L. "Cleveland's Personality as a Political Leader." *The Psycho-
   analytic Review* 51 no. 2 (1964): 130-54.
Robinson, Paul A. "Romantic Sexual Theory," paper read at the annual conven-
   tion of the American Historical Association, Dec. 29, 1970 at Boston, Mass.
Rogow, Arnold, *James Forrestal: A Study of Personality Politics and Policy.* NY:
   Macmillan, 1963.
———. "Private Illness and Public Policy: The Case of James Forrestal and John
   Winnant." *American Journal of Psychiatry* 125 (1969): 1093-98.
Rohleder, Hermann. "Das Sexuelle im Leben Napoleon I." *Sexualprobleme,*
   Feb., 1913.
Rosen, Edward. "Kepler's Attitude to His Mother." *Psychoanalytic Review* 55
   (1968): 342-48.
Rosen, George. *Madness in Society.* Chicago: Univ. of Chicago Press, 1968.
Rothstein, David. "The Presidential Assassination Syndrome: Application to Lee
   Harvey Oswald." *Archives of General Psychiatry,* 15 (1966): 260-66.
———. "Presidential Assassination Syndrome." *Ibid.,* 11 (1964): 245-54.

Sachs, Hans. "Ein Traum Bismarcks." *Internationale Zeitschrift für ärtzliche
   Psychoanalyse* 1 (1913): 80-83.
St. Ehrlich, Vera. *Family in Transition: A Study of 300 Yugoslav Villages.*
   Princeton, N.J.: Princeton Univ. Press, 1966.
Saussure, Raymond De. "Collective Neuroses of Germany." *Free World* 5 (1943):
   121-26.
———. "Hitler et l'Allemagne." *Pour la Victoire,* January 10, 1943.
———. "L'Inconnu chez Hitler." *Les Oevres Nouvelles* 2 (1943): 178-244.
Schalk, David L. "The Character of Louis XV." *American Imago* 19 (1962):
   425-35.
Schoenwald, Richard L. "Town Guano and 'Social Statics,'" *Victorian Studies*
   11 Supplement (1968): 691-710. .
———. "Training Urban Man: A Hypothesis About the Sanitary Movement." in
   H. J. Dyos and M. Wolf, eds., *The Victorian City.* London, 1973, 2:669-92.
Schupper, Fabian X and Roy C. Calogeras. "Psycho-Cultural Shifts in Ego De-
   fenses." *American Imago* 28 (1971): 53-70.
Siegel, J. E. "Marx's Early Development: Vocation, Rebellion, and Realism."
   Journal of Interdisciplinary History 3 (1972): 391-418.
Sempell, Charlotte. "Bismarck's Childhood: A Psychohistorical Study." *History*

of Childhood Quarterly 2 (1974): 107-24.

Sennett, Richard. *Families Against the City: Middle Class Homes of Industrial Chicago, 1872-1890*. Cambridge, Mass.: Harvard Univ. Press, 1970.

Shannon, David. "Woodrow Wilson's Youth and Personality: An Essay Review." *Pacific Northwest Quarterly*, 58 (1967): 205-07.

Shore, Miles F. "Henry VIII and the Crisis of Generativity." *The Journal of Interdisciplinary History* 2 (1972): 359-90.

Shorter, Edward. "Illegitimacy, Sexual Revolution and Social Change in Modern Europe." *Journal of Interdisciplinary History* 2 (1972): also in *The American Family in Socio-Historical Perspective*. Ed. by Michael Gordon. NY: St. Martin's Press, 1974.

Silverberg, William V. "Race Prejudice—Social Immaturity." *Current History* 5 (1943): 25-29.

Simon, Bennett and Nancy. "The Pacifist Turn: An Episode of Mystic Illumination in the Autobiography of Bertrand Russell." *Journal of the American Psychoanalytic Association* 20 (1972): 109-21.

Simpson, George. *People in Families: Sociology, Psychoanalysis, and the American Family*. NY: Thomas Y. Crowell, 1960.

Sleigh, Alfred. "Hitler: A Study in Megalomania." *Canadian Psychiatric Association Journal* 11 (1966): 218-19.

Slochower, Harry. "Hitler's 'Elevation' of the Jew: Ego-Splitting and Ego-Function." *American Imago* 28 (1971): 304-318.

Smith, Bradley F. *Adolf Hitler: His Family, Childhood and Youth*. Stanford, Cal.: Stanford Univ, 1967.

Smith, Louis. "Aaron Burr." *Psychoanalytic Quarterly* 12 (1943): 67-99.

Smith-Rosenberg, Carroll. "Volition, Aggression and Conflict: Hysteria as a Female Social Role," paper read at the annual convention of the Organization of American Historians, April 12, 1973, at Chicago, Ill.

Spindle, Dearborn. "American Character as Revealed by the Military." *Psychiatry*, 11 (1949): 275-83.

Stampp, Kenneth. "Rebels and Sambos: The Search for the Negro's Personality in Slavery." *Journal of Southern History* 37 (1971): 367-92.

Sterba, Edith and Richard. *Beethoven and His Nephew: A Psychoanalytic Study of Their Relationship*. London: Dennis Dobson, 1957.

Sterba, Richard. "Some Psychological Factors in Negro Race Hatred and in Anti-Negro Riots." *Psychoanalysis and the Social Sciences* 1 (1947): 411-27.

Storr, Anthony. "The Man." In *Churchill Revised: A Critical Assessment*, pp. 229-74. Ed. by A. J. Taylor, et al. NY: Dial Press, 1969.

Talmon, J. L. "The Ordeal of Sir Lewis Namier: The Man, the Historian, the Jew." *Commentary* 33 (1962): 237-46.

Thorpe, Earl E. *Eros and Freedom in Southern Life and Thought*. Durham, N.C.: Seeman Bindery, 1967.

———. *The Old South: A Psychohistory*. Durham, N.C.: Seeman Bindery, 1972.

Tompkins, Sylvia S. "The Psychology of Commitment: The Constructive Role of Violence and Suffering for the Individual and His Society," in Martin B. Duberman, ed., *The Antislavery Vanguard: New Essays on the Abolitionists*. Princeton, N.J., Princeton Univ. Press, 1963: 270-300.

Tramer, M. "Das Kind der Masse." *Zeitschrift für Kinderpsychiatrie* 13 (1947): 221-32.

Tucker, Robert C. "The Dictator and Totalitarianism." *World Politics* 17 (1965): 555-83.

———. *Stalin as Revolutionary, 1879-1929: A Study in History and Personality*. NY: W. W. Norton, 1973.

Umansky, Howard. "The Roosevelt Family: Three Generations of Sibling Rivalry," paper read at the annual convention of the American Historical Association, Dec. 29, 1973, at San Francisco, Calif.

Van Clute, Walton. "How Fascism Thwarts the Life Instinct: An Application of Psychoanalysis to Current Political Phenomena." *American Journal of Orthopsychiatry* 12 (1942): 335-37.

Veith, Ilza. "English Melancholy and American Nervousness." *Bulletin of the Menninger Clinic*, 32 (1968): 301-17.

Volkan, Varnik D. "The Birds of Cyprus: A Psycho-political Observation." *American Journal of Psychotherapy* 26 (1972): 378-83.

Waite, Robert G. L. "Adolf Hitler's Antisemitism: A Study in History and Psychoanalysis." In *The Psychoanalytic Interpretation of History*. Ed. by Benjamin B. Wolman. NY: Basic Books, 1971.

———. "Adolf Hitler's Guilt Feelings: A Problem in History and Psychology." *The Journal of Interdisplinary History* 1 (1971): 229-250.

Walters, Ronald G. "Anti-Slavery and Sexuality," paper read at the annual convention of the Organization of American Historians, April 15, 1971, at New Orleans, La.

Wangh, Martin. "National Socialism and the Genocide of the Jews, a Psycho-Analytic Study of a Historical Event." *International Journal of Psycho-Analysis* 45 (1964): 386-98.

———. "A Psychoanalytic Study of Antisemitism: The Psychodynamics and Psychogenesis of Prejudice, Anti-Semitism, and Nazi Anti-Semitism." Read at New York Psycho-Analytic Society, Oct. 30, 1962.

———. "Psychoanalytische Betrachtungen zur Dynamik u. Genese des Vorurteils, des Antisemitismus und des Nazismus." *Psyche* 6 (1962): 273-84.

*Ward, Dana. "Kissinger: A Psychohistory." *History of Childhood Quarterly* 2 (1975): 287-349.

Waters, John J. "James Otis, Jr.: An Ambivalent Revolutionary." *History of Childhood Quarterly* 1 (1973): 142-50.

Weinstein, Edwin Alexander. "Denial of Presidential Disability: A Case Study of Woodrow Wilson." *Psychiatry* 30 (1967): 376-91.

———. "Wilson's Neurological Illness." *Journal of American History* 57 (1970): 339-51.

——— and Olga Lyerly. "Symbolic Aspects of Presidential Assassination." *Psychiatry*, 32 (1969): 1-11.

Weinstein, Fred and Platt, Gerald M. *The Wish to be Free: Society, Psyche, and Value Change*. Berkeley/L.A.: Univ of Calif. Press, 1969.

*Weissman, Philip. "Why Booth Killed Lincoln: A Psychoanalytic Study of a Historical Tragedy." In *Psychological Studies of Famous Americans: The Civil War Era*. Ed. by Norman Kiell. NY: Twayne, 1964.

Wellman, Judith and Barbara Gerber. "Out of the Wilderness: A Psychosocial Odyssey of Sarah and Angelina Grimke, 1792-1836," paper read at the annual convention of the Organization of American Historials, April 1974 at Denver, Colo.

Wilkinson, Burke. *Young Louis Fourteenth: The Early Years of the Sun King*. Riverside, N.J.: Macmillan Publ. Co., Inc., 1970.

Willcox, William B. *Portrait of a General: Sir Henry Clinton in the War of Independence*. NY: Knopf, 1964.

Williams, Margaret T., "Psychoanalysis and Latin American History." In Richard Graham and Peter H. Smith, eds., *New Approaches to Latin American History*. Austin, Texas: Univ. of Texas Press, 1975.

Wilson, George W. "John Wilkes Booth: Father Murdered." *American Imago* 1 (1940): 49-60.

———. "A Prophetic Dream Reported by Abraham Lincoln." *American Imago* 1 (1940): 42-48. Also in *Psychological Studies of Famous Americans*. Ed. by Norman Kiell. NY: Twayne, 1964.

Wolf, Howard R. "British Fathers and Sons, 1773-1913: From Filial Submissiveness to Creativity." *Psychoanalysis and the Psychoanalytic Review* 52 (1965): 197-214.

Wolfenstein, E. Victor. *The Revolutionary Personality: Lenin, Trotsky and Gandhi*. Princeton, N.J.: Princeton Univ. Press, 1967.

Wolff, Michael. "Victorian Study: An Interdisciplinary Essay." *Victorian Studies* 8 no. 1 (1964): 59-70.

Woodward, C. Vann. "John Brown's Private War." In *Psychological Studies of Famous Americans*. Ed. by Norman Kiell. NY: Twayne, 1964.

Wyatt, F. and Wilcox, W. B. "Sir Henry Clinton: A Psychological Exploration in History." *William and Mary Quarterly* ser 3 16 (Jan, 1959): 3-26.

Young, Michael and Willmott, Peter. *Family and Kinship in East London.* NY: Humanities Press, Inc., 1957.

Zeligs, Meyer A. *Friendship to Fratricide: An Analysis of Whitaker Chambers and Alger Hiss.* NY: Viking Press, 1967.
Zilboorg, Gregory. *The Passing of the Old Order in Europe.* NY: T. Seltzer, 1920.
Zink, Harold. "A Case Study of a Political Boss." *Psychiatry* 1 (1938): 527-33.

VI. ASIA

Adatia, M. D. "Child-Parent Relationship." *Journal of Indian Medical Profession* 4 (1958): 2081-83; 2089.
All India Educational Conference on Human Affairs, 16th. *The Influence of the Home on the Child.* Udipi, India, 1944.
Alpert, Augusta. "Dasgupta Jnanendra: Behavior Problems of School Children." *Psychoanalytic Quarterly* 18 (1949): 393-94.

Behramji, Malabara. *Infant Marriage and Enforced Widowhood in India.* Reprint of 1887 ed. Ann Arbor, Mich.: The Finch Press, n.d.
Benedict, Ruth Fulton. *The Chrysanthemum and the Sword.* Boston, 1946.
Bose, Nirmal Kumar. "Some Facts of Psychoanalytic Interest of Gandhiji's Life." *Samsika* 6 (1952): 163-75.
Bychowski, Gustav. "A Brief Visit to India: Observations and Psychoanalytic Implications." *American Imago* 25 no. 1 (1968): 59-76.

Caudill, William and Helen Weinstein. "Maternal Care and Infant Behavior in Japan and America." *Psychiatry* 32 (1969): 12-43.
Choisy, Maryse. "Gandhi dans le monde Modern." *Psyche,* Paris 3 (1948): 2-12.

Droppers, Garrett. "The Population of Japan in the Tokugawa Period." *Transactions of the Asiatic Society of Japan* XXI (1894): 253-84.

Embree, Ainslie T. "Studies in Indian History." *The Journal of Interdisciplinary History* 2 no. 4 (1972): 477-82.
Erikson, Erik H. "Gandhi's Autobiography: The Leader as a Child." *The American Scholar* (Autumn, 1966).
———. *Gandhi's Truth.* NY: Norton, 1969.

Fisher, Margaret and Sutherland, J. D. "Gandhi: A Psychoanalytic View." *American Historical Review* 76 (1971): 1104-115.
Freedman, Maurice, ed. *Family and Kinship in Chinese Society.* Stanford, Cal.: Stanford Univ. Press, 1970.
Friedman, Lawrence. "Japan and the Psychopathology of History." *Psychoanalytic Quarterly* 37 (1968): 539-64.
Frost, Peter K. "Men of Meiji: The Possibility of Japanese Psychobiography," *Journal of Interdisciplinary History,* III (1973): 581-584.

Grazia, Sebastian de. "Mahatma Gandhi: The Son of His Mother." *Political Quarterly* 19 (1948): 336-48.
Gupta, G. R. *Marriage, Religion and Society: Tradition and Change in an Indian Village.* NY: Halsted Press, 1973.
Gupta, N. N. "Influence of Hindu Culture and Social Customs on Psychosomatic Disease in India." *Psychosomatic Review* 18 (1956): 506-10.

Haring, Douglas G. "Japanese National Character: Cultural Anthropology, Psychoanalysis, and History." In *Personal Character and Cultural Milieu.* Ed. by Douglas G. Harding. Syracuse: Syracuse Univ. Press, 1956.

Honjo, Eijiro. "The Population and its Problems in the Tokugawa Era." *Bulletin de l'Institut International de Statistique* XXV no. 2 (1931): 60-82.
Howes, John F. "Uchimura Kanzo: Japanese Prophet." In Dankwart A. Rustow, ed., *Philosophers and Kinds: Studies in Leadership.* NY: George Braziller, 1970: 180-207.
Hsu, Francis L. K. *Under the Ancestors' Shadow: Chinese Culture and Personality.* NY, 1948.

Ishii, Ryoichi. *Population Pressure and Economic Life in Japan.* London, 1937.

Jones, Kenneth W. "Anxiety and Identity: The Creation of a Hindu Consciousness," paper read at the annual convention of the American Historical Assoc. Dec. 28, 1974, at Chicago, Ill.

Kapru, Promilla. *Marriage and the Working Woman in India.* Mystic, Conn.: Verry, Lawrence, Inc., 1970.
Keddie, Nikki R. "Sayyid Jamal ad-Din 'al-Afghani': A Case of Post humous Charisma? In Dankwart A. Rustow, ed., *Philosophers and Kings: Studies in Leadership.* NY: George Braziller, 1970: 148-79.
Kondo, Akhihisa. "Intuition in Zen Buddhism." *American Journal of Psychoanalysis* 12 (1952): 10-14.

Lanham, Betty. "Aspects of Child Care in Japan: Preliminary Report." In *Personal Character and Cultural Milieu.* Ed. by Douglas G. Haring. Syracuse: Syracuse Univ. Press, 1956.
Lifton, R. J. "Individual Patterns and Historical Change: Imagery of Japanese Youth." *Journal of Social Issues* 20 (1964): 96-111.
——. *Revolutionary Immortality: Mao-Tse-tung and the Chilese Cultural Revolution.* NY: Vintage, 1968.
——. *Thought Reform and the Psychology of Totalism: A Study of "Brainwashing in China.* NY: Norton, 1963.

Madan, Kashmir T. N. *Family and Kinship: A Study of the Pandits of Rural Kashmir.* NY: Asia Publishing House, Inc., 1965.
Masson-Oursel, Paul. "Gandhi Assassiné." *Psyché-Paris* 3 (1948): 13-14.
Maupin, Edward W. "Zen Buddhism: A Psychological Review." *Journal of Consult. Psychology* 26 (1962): 362-78.
Moloney, James C. *Understanding the Japanese Mind.* NY: Greenwood Press, 1968.
Moor, Edward. *Hindu Infanticide.* London, 1811.
Muensterberger, Warner. "Orality and Dependence: Characteristics of Southern Chinese." *Psychoanalysis and the Social Sciences* 3, 1951.

Norbeck, Edward and Margaret. "Child Training in a Japanese Fishing Community." In *Personal Character and Cultural Milieu.* Syracuse: Syracuse Univ. Press, 1956.

Palátre, P. *L'Infanticide el l'oeuvre de la Sainte-Enfance en Chine.* Shanghai, 1878.
Panigrahi, Lalita. *British Social Policy and Female Infanticide in India.* New Delhi, 1972.
Ping-ti, Ho. *Studies in the Population of China, 1368-1953.* Cambridge, Mass., 1959.
Pomper, Philip. Review Essay of Erik H. Erikson's 'Gandhi's Truth.' " NY: W. W. Norton & Co., 1969. *History and Theory* 9 (1970): 202-09.
Pye, Lucien W. *Politics, Personality and Nation Building: Burma's Search for Identity.* New Haven: Yale Univ. Press,.1962.
——. *The Spirit of Chinese Politics: A Psychocultural Study of the Authority of Crisis in Political Development.* Cambridge, Mass.: M.I.T. Press, 1968.

Raddock, David M. "Growing Up in New China: A Twist in the Circle of Filial Piety." *History of Childhood Quarterly* 2 (1974): 201-20.
Rustow, Dankwart A. "Atatürk as Founder of a State." In Dankwart A. Rustow, ed., *Philosophers and Kings: Studies in Leadership.* NY: Braziller, 1970: 208-47.

45

Schneiderman, Leo. "Ramakrishna: Personality and Social Factors in the Growth of a Religious Movement." *J. for Scientific Study of Rel.* 8 (1969): 60-81.

Sidel, Ruth. *Women and Child Care in China.* NY: Hill and Wang, 1972.

Sikkema, Mildred. "Observations on Japanese Early Child Training." *Psychiatry* 10 (1947): 423-32.

Srya, Subhash, C. *Infant and Child Care for the Indian Mother.* NY: International Publications Service, 1970.

Taeuber, Irene B. *The Population of Napan.* Princeton, 1958.

Tseng, Weu-Shing. "The Conflict of Personality in Confucian Thought." *Psychiatry* 36 (1973): 191-202.

Wilson, John. *History of the Suppression of Infanticide in Western India.* Bombay, 1855.

Wolf, Arthur P. "Childhood Association, Sexual Attraction and the Incest Taboo: A Chinese Case." *American Anthropologist* 68 (1966): 882-894.

Wolf, Margery. "Child Training and the Chinese Family." In *Family and Kinship in Chinese Society.* Ed. by Maurice Freedman. Stanford: Stanford Univ. Press, 1970.

———. *The House of Lim: A Study of a Chinese Farm Family.* NY: Appleton-Century-Crofts, 1968.

———. *Women and the Family in Rural Taiwan.* Stanford: Stanford Univ. Press, 1972.

Wright, Arthur F. "Sui Yang-Ti: Personality and Stereotype." In *Confucianism and Chilese Civilization.* Ed. by Arthur F. Wright. NY: Antheneum, 1965.

APPENDIX:
A GUIDE TO THE INTERDISCIPLINARY LITERATURE OF THE HISTORY OF CHILDHOOD

MANUEL D.
LOPEZ

ARRANGEMENT

Interdisciplinary research is, in fact, a courageous undertaking. A researcher finds among his smaller problems: specialized usage of common terms, a confusion of meanings due to an overlapping of concepts, and frustration compounded by lack of familiarity with the literatures and sources of information of those fields beyond his original discipline. Depending upon his orientation, he discovers, according to the field of endeavor, a variety of bibliographic tools representing a wide spectrum of sophistication and reflecting, usually, the particular needs and biases of the scholars and practitioners within particular fields.

The guide presented is of a general nature; the effort here is only to provide examples of the basic bibliographic instruments available as well as the diversity of possible approaches. The arrangement of the entries is by form (Abstracts, Indexes, Bibliographies, Encyclopedias, Dictionaries, Handbooks) or by content (Dissertations and Theses, Biographical Sources, Directories, Manuscripts, Subject Collections and Specialized Sources, Book Reviews, Newspapers, Government Publications and Graphics). Within each category the sequence of citation is from the general to the specific, the comprehensive to the particular or from the current to the retrospective.

From a specialist's viewpoint, this guide is inadequate—and his criticism is valid in relation to his specialty; however, this effort is directed toward the non-specialist. Hopefully, this guide will provide the basis for the expansion, modification and emphasis that will meet the needs of the individual investigator. Even if this guide should meet the current needs of some scholars, bibliographic aids are dated almost as soon as they are completed. To maintain such a resource, a card file with appropriate form or subject headings could be developed. As publications of value appear they could be noted with comments concerning their scope, arrangement, omissions, special features such as charts, indexes and bibliographies, and some indication of the particular value of each item.

Manuel D. Lopez is reference librarian with the Lockwood Memorial Library, State University of New York at Buffalo, and has published widely in the area of bibliographic control and access.

BIBLIOGRAPHIES

A1   White, Carl Milton
    Sources of information in the Social Sciences: a guide to the literature [by] Carl M. White and associates. [Totawa, N.J.] Bedminister Press [1964].

48

The specific disciplines of history, business administration and economics, anthropology, psychology, political science, sociology and the general literature of the social sciences are within the scope of this bibliographic guide. An introduction to each field and a review and evaluation of basic monographic works in English.

A2   *U.S. Library of Congress*
Library of Congress Catalog; a cumulative list of works represented by Library of Congress printed cards. Books: subjects. Jan/Mar. 1950-   , Washington.
Quarterly issues, an annual and quinquennial cumulation. Entries in this excellent subject bibliography are for items with an imprint date of 1945 or later which have been cataloged. Materials included are pamphlets, atlases, serials, periodicals, maps and books in all languages.

A3   *The British national bibliography.* 1950-
A weekly list of new British books received by the Agent for the Copyright Libraries. Arranged by Dewey classification. Each weekly list contains an author and title index. The final weekly list for the month contains separate author and subject indexes. Weekly lists are cumulated for the periods January-April, May-August and an annual cumulation for January-December. Since 1950 there have been cumulative author, subject and title volumes for periods of 3 to 5 years.

Note: Other national bibliographies of interest and value: *Canadiana,* 1950-   ; *Bibliografia nazionale italiana,* 1958- ; *Bibliographie de la France; journal général de l'imprimerie et de la librarie,* v; 1-   , 1811-   ; and *Les Livres de l'année,* 1933-1938, 1946/48-   .

A4   *Cumulative book index,* 1928-   , New York (etc.) W. H. Wilson Co.
Monthly issues except July, August and December, cumulating at irregular intervals. Useful bibliography with the limitation of including only English language material. Books listed under author, subject and title.

A5   U.S. Department of Health, Education and Welfare. Library.
Author/Title catalog of the department library, Boston, G. K. Hall, 1965, v. 1-29.
An alphabetic arrangement, by author and title, of some 850,000 entries for this collection of 500,000 volumes composed of books, papers, pamphlets proceedings, local, state and federal documents. Particularly strong in the areas of the social sciences and education. This catalog is an invaluable resource when trying to identify a government publication by title or author.

A6   ——————. *Subject catalog of the department library*
Boston, G. K. Hall, 1965, v. 1-20.
Approximately 350,000 subject cards for government documents, pamphlets, serial publications and books. The current cat-

alog is the product of combining an "Education Catalog" and a "Social Welfare Catalog" each with its own subject approach. The problems generated by merging the two systems have been reduced by an extensive use of cross references and "see references".

A7　Aldous, Joan
　　　International bibliography of research in marriage and the family, 1900-1964 ... [Minneapolis] Distributed by the University of Minnesota Press for the Minnesota Family Study Center and the Institute of Life Insurance [1967].
　　　References (12,850) are to monographs, journals, books, pamphlets, parts of books, bulletins and fugitive publications; the goal was to "list every research item published since 1900 in which some manifestation of marriage or the family figures". Preface contains an extensive list of exclusions. The variety of access includes a key word index, a subject index, a list of authors, a list of titles and a final section that has full bibliographic citations for each item.

A8　*Bibliographic index; a cumulative bibliography of bibliographies.*
　　　(v.　) 11, New York, the H. W. Wilson Co., 1945
　　　A comprehensive semiannual subject index to bibliographies that have appeared in books and pamphlets as well as some 1900 periodicals that are systematically covered. To be cited a bibliography must have at least 40 entries.

A9　*Essay and general literature index; an index to essays and articles in ... collections of essays and miscellaneous works.* v. 1-　,
　　　1900-1933—
　　　A subject, author, and when relevant, title index to essays, chapters and parts of books that are in collections of essays and miscellaneous works. This bibliographic resource performs the same function for books as a periodical index does for the journal literature. A semiannual publication that cumulates annually and quinquennially. The 1971 volume states, "An index of 4,223 essays and articles in 252 volumes of collections of essays and miscellaneous works."

A10　Evans, Charles, 1850-1935
　　　American bibliography, by Charles Evans. A chronological dictionary of all books, pamphlets and periodical publications printed in the United States of America from the genesis of printing in 1639 down to and including the year 1820. With bibliographical and biographical notes ... Chicago, Priv. print. for the author by the Blakely Press, 1903-1959. Chronological arrangement, numbered continuously. There is a classified subject index, an author index and a list of publishers and printers. Actually only complete through 1800, volume 13 covering the years 1799-1800. Volume 14 is an author-title index to the set.

Note: Similar publications are: Shaw, R. & Shoemaker, R. A., *American Bibliography;* Historical Records Survey, *American Imprints Inventory.*

A11 Bristol, Roger Pattrell
Supplement to Charles Evans' American Bibliography. Charlottesville. Published for the Bibliographical Society of America and the Bibliographical Society of Virginia [by] University Press of Virginia [1970].
Over 11,000 items—books, pamphlets, broadsides, journals, newspapers and ephemera—printed in America between 1639-1800 but not included in Evans. Arranged chronologically, entries include citations to bibliographies and library locations.

——————.
Index to Supplement to Charles Evans' American Bibliography
Charlottesville. Published for the Bibliographical Society of the University of Virginia [by the] University Press of Virginia [1971].
Two indexes: 1) Authors and titles; 2) Printers, publishers and booksellers.

A12 *Early American Imprints*
First Series (Evans) 1639-1800. Readex Microprint Corp.
This is a microprint edition of over 42,000 titles, reproduced in full, that are listed in Evans' *American Bibliography.*

A13 *Early American Imprints*
Second Series (Shaw-Shoemaker), 1801-1819. Readex Microprint Corp.
About 50,000 titles (books, pamphlets, broadsides) printed in the U.S. between 1801-1819 are reproduced in full.
These two microfilm collections are available in a number of libraries thus providing the scholar with ready access to rare and unusual primary materials.

A14 Pollard, Alfred William, 1859-   comp.
A short-title catalogue of books printed in England, Scotland and Ireland and of English books printed abroad, 1475-1640. Compiled by A. W. Pollard & G. R. Redgrave, with the help of G. F. Barwick, George Watson Cole, Ethel Fegan . . . and others. London, The Bibliographical Society, 1926.
A catalogue of books, giving the location of copies (usually 3 in the United Kingdom, 3 in the U.S.); arranged alphabetically by author's name. Entry numbers facilitate the cross reference system.
"English" is defined to include every book, regardless of language printed in England, Wales and Scotland. Works by English authors printed out of England in languages other than English are excluded.

A15 Wing, Donald Goddard, 1904-
Short-title catalogue of books printed in England, Scotland, Ireland, Wales, and British America, and of English books printed

in other countries, 1641-1700. New York, Index Society, 1945-51. Some 90,000 abridged entries for books, "copies of which are known to exist." The locations, a maximum of 10 (5 in the United Kingdom and 5 in the U.S.) of copies are provided when possible. Works by English authors printed outside England in a language other than English have been excluded. Trials are listed by title; pamphlets of less than fifty pages are so indicated. Each main entry has an entry number composed by a letter and number. The arrangement is alphabetical by author; material by anonymous and pseudonymous authors should be searched by the first word of the title.

Such short-title catalogs as Wing's and the one by Pollard are not unique. Other catalogues have been produced related to other countries and time periods.

A16 *Early English Books*

The availability of the items cited in Pollard and Redgrave *Short-Title Catalogue* has been expanded by a project to microfilm those titles. *Early English Books, 1475-1640,* started in 1938 and is currently in progress. A similar project, *Early English Books, 1641-1700,* exists for the material listed in *Wing's Short-Title Catalogue.*

N.B. Similar publications include the British Museum's Dept. of Printed Books' *Short-title catalogue of books printed in France and of French Books printed in other countries from 1470 to 1600 in the British Museum; Short title catalogue of books printed in Italy and of Italian books printed in other countries from 1495-1600 now in the British Museum; Short-title catalogue of books printed in the German speaking countries and German books printed in other countries from 1455-1600 now in the British Museum; Short-title catalogue of books printed in the Netherlands and Belgium and of Dutch and Flemish books printed in other countries from 1470 to 1600 now in the British Museum; Short-title catalogues of Spanish, Spanish-American and Portuguese books printed before 1601 in the British Museum.* Other examples include Herbert Mayow Adams' *Catalogue of books printed on the continent of Europe, 1501-1600 in Cambridge libraries; Bibliographie der deutschen Drucke des XVI. Jahrhunderts, 1960-* ; the Hispanic Society of America's *Printed books, 1468-1700, in the Hispanic Society of America,* J. Brucker's *A Bibliographical catalogue of seventeenth-century German books published in Holland.*

AUTOBIOGRAPHY AND BIOGRAPHY

B1 *Biography index; a cumulative index to biographical materials in books and magazines.* 1-   , Jan. 1946/July 1949-

Cumulating annually, this quarterly is an index to biographical material including collections of letters, diaries, obituaries, memoirs and bibliographies, that has been cited in periodicals, individual and collective biographies and other non-biographical books. Main section: biographies are arranged alphabetically, this section is followed by a list of biographies arranged by profession or occupation. Biographies, other than American, are so indicated. No limit regarding nationality or time period.

Note: Sources of biographical information among others include: *Webster's Biographical Dictionary* (1966); *Dictionary of American Biography* (1928-   ); *Dictionary of National Biography* (1885-   ); *Dictionnaire Biographique francais contemporain* (1950-   ); and the *Österreichesches biographisches Lexikon, 1815-1950*. Graz, H. Böhlaus Nachf... 1957 (1954-   ); *Dizionario biografico degli italiani*. Rome (1960-   ).

B2   Jöcher, Christian Gottlieb, 1694-1758.
Allgemeines Gelehrten–Lexicon. Hildeshein, G. Olms, 1751-51. Repr. 1961
Bibliographical sketches of individuals before 1750, covers all time periods and nationalities. Particularly good for Middle ages. Sources are given with extensive bibliographies.

—————.
Fortsetzung und Ergänzungen zum Allgemeinem Gelehrten-Lexicon... von Johan Christoph Adelung. Hindeshein, G. Olms, 1960.
Supplement has essentially same scope as well as some material of a later date.

B3   *Biographie universelle (Michaud) ancienne et moderne.* Nouv. éd. publiée sous la direction de M. Michaud, rev., corr, et considérablement augm. d'articles omis ou nouveaux; ouvrage rédigé par une société de gens de lettres et de savants. Paris, Mme. C. Desplaces, 1843-65.
Signed articles with bibliographies, considered the most important of the large dictionaries of universal biography.

B4   Phillips, Lawrence B.
Dictionary of biographical reference; containing over one hundred thousand names together with a classed index of the biographical literature of Europe and America. New edition rev., corr, and augm. with supplement to date, by Frank Weitenkampf. (3rd ed.) London, Law, Philadelphia, Gebbie, 1889.
International in scope, covers all periods, entries providing full names, dates and references to biographical collections. Bibliography of biography arranged: 1) general biographies according to language; 2) national biographies arranged by country and subdivided into provinces and cities; 3) by subject, occupation, activity: i.e., knights, athiests, popes, suicides, etc.

B5   Misch, Georg
      A History of autobiography in antiquity (translated in collaboration with the author by E. W. Dickes). Cambridge, Mass., Harvard University Press, 1951.
      ". . . autobiographies demand for their appreciation . . . a comprehensive view of the development of the human mind." Starting with a ". . . consideration of the growth of man's awareness of personality" volume one examines the conception and origin of autobiography, its form in the ancient Middle East, its development in post-Homeric Greece and in the Hellenistic and Greco-Roman world. Volume two explores autobiographical writings in religious and philosophical movements up to and including the Middle Ages. With reference to specific individuals, autobiography is explored from the viewpoints: politics, the "confessional", and character analysis. Volume 2 has the index for both volumes. Extensive notes provide additional and perceptive reference to primary sources and commentary.

B6   ——————.
      Geschichte der Autobiographie. 3rd ed. Frankfurt, 1949-69.
      Eight volume study of autobiography in various relationships to art, literature, religion, culture, etc., from antiquity to the nineteenth century. Each volume has its own name and subject index.

B7   Acta sanctorum
      Acta sanctorum quotquot toto orbe coluntur, vel a catholicis scriptoribus celebrantur quae ex Latinis et Graecis, aliarumque gentium antiquis monumentis collegit, digessit, notis illustravit Ioannes Bollandus . . . Editio novissima curante Joanne Carnandet . . . Paris, v. Palmé 1863-1940 84 V. in 67.
      First publication dated 1643. For an account of this publication that continued for three hundred years see the *Catholic Encyclopedia.* 2:630-39.

B8   *Bibliotheca sanctorum*
      [Roma] Instituto Giovanni XXIII nella Pontificia Università lateranense [1961?–   ].
      Signed biographical sketches that vary in length from one column to three pages. Bibliography for each entry. Four indexes: 1) by saint, 2) according to saint's day, according to a variety of calendars, 3) according to patronage (feast day, functions association with cities and towns, date of sanctification, etc.), 4) by author of articles.

      Analecta bollandiana
      Société des Bollandistes, V. 1, –1882–
      Texts, commentaries, and critical reviews of new publications about the lives of saints. Actually supplements *Acta sanctorum.*

B9   Lillard, Richard Gordon
      American life in autobiography, a descriptive guide. Stanford,
      Calif., Stanford University Press, 1956.
      Over four hundred volumes written by Americans and printed
      since 1900. Classified arrangement by occupation, a general index
      provides rapid access. Annotations emphasize the style, reader ap-
      peal and general contents of the autobiography.

B10   Hefling, Helen
      *Hefling & Richards' Index to contemporary biography and
      criticism.* A new ed. rev. and ent. by Helen Hefling . . . and Jessie
      W. Dyde . . . with an introduction by Miss Mary Emogene
      Hazeltine. Boston, F. W. Faxon Company, 1934.
      Indexes 417 titles concerning individuals born later than 1850.
      Many individuals have multiple citations.

B11   O'Neill, Edward Hayes
      Biography by Americans, 1658-1936; a subject bibliography by
      Edward H. O'Neill. Philadelphia, University of Pennsylvania Press;
      London, H. Milford, Oxford University Press, 1939.
      Some seven thousand biographies arranged alphabetically by
      the biographees name in part I. Part II cites the collected biog-
      raphies by the compiler's name. Excluded are autobiographies,
      diaries and journals, however, this bibliography attempts to "note
      every known biography" and "covers every possible field of life."

B12   Kaplan, Louis
      A Bibliography of American autobiographies. Madison, Uni-
      versity of Wisconsin Press, 1961.
      Six thousand three hundred and seventy seven autobiographies
      including those of Americans who lived abroad as well as foreign
      authors who lived in the U.S. for an "appreciable period." Ex-
      cludes works that were published after 1945, fiction, diaries,
      journals and letters. Arranged alphabetically by the name of the
      author, each entry contains bibliographic information and the lo-
      cation of a copy in a library. A very detailed index including a
      chronological listing by period.

B13   Matthews, William
      *British autobiographies; an annotated bibliography of British
      autobiographies published or written before 1951.* Berkeley, Uni-
      versity of California Press, 1955.
      About four thousand autobiographies concerned with a "sig-
      nificant" segment of the life of an author who "seemed to be
      mostly concerned with himself". Brief characterization of the
      book-persons, places, and subjects. Arrangement is alphabetical by
      name of the writer. British is "born in the British Isles" and
      "naturalized British Subject", although titles concerned with life
      in the colonies are not excluded. Autobiographies of life lived in
      U.S., Canada, South Africa, Australia, New Zealand and auto-

biographies of Indians are excluded. An index by occupation, profession, places, regions, wars, and general topics gives ready access. N.B. Colonial diaries are included.

B14 Stauffer, Donald Alfred
English biography before 1700, by ... Cambridge, Mass., Harvard University Press, 1930.

Essentially a study, historically and critically, of the art of English biography. Index-subject and author of early English biographies (pp. 289-366). "A list of the most important work of reference for the study of early English biography" requires pp. 367-372. A standard index of biographers, biographies and sources complete the volume.

B15 Royal Commonwealth Society Library.
Biography catalogue of the Library of the Royal Commonwealth Society, By Donald H. Simpson, librarian. London, Royal Commonwealth Society, 1961.

Includes biographies, autobiographies, personal accounts of particular events, and accounts of artists and writers published up to 1960, of individuals born in or connected with the Commonwealth countries or individuals of the U.K. significantly involved in Imperial Affairs. The definition of inclusion is sufficiently broad to cite biographies of travellers and explorers of many nations as well as entries relating to Colonial America.

B16 Bode, Ingrid
Die Autobiographien zur deutschen Literatur, Kunst und Musik 1900-1965; Bibliographie und Nachweise der persönlichen Begegnungen und Charakteristiken. Stuttgart, Metzler [1966].

Some 500 autobiographies including significant diaries are cited with full bibliographic data. Each entry identifies the author and notes indicate the time span covered, persons, places and events. A separate index to individuals, cited in the autobiographies. A second index by profession provides a subject approach to this excellent bibliography.

N.B. For studies of the history, form and value of autobiography and biography see Anna Robeson Burr's *The Autobiography* (1909); Waldo Hilary Dunn's *English Biography* (1966) and John Mark Longaker's *English Biography in the Eighteenth Century* (1931).

DIARIES AND LETTERS

C1 Forbes, Harriette (Merrifield) 1856-1951, comp.
New England diaries, 1602-1800, a descriptive catalogue of diaries, orderly books and sea journals. New York, Pursell & Pursell, 1923.

Diaries, orderly books and sea journals kept by either residents of New England or strangers writing of their experiences in New England. Three separate sections according to form. The entries include brief identifying biographical data, notes concerning ownership, location of manuscript and publication information.

C2   Matthews, William
American diaries; an annotated bibliography of American diaries written prior to the year 1861, compiled by William Matthews . . . Berkeley, University of California Press, 1945.

Limited to published diaries written in the English language by Americans and Canadians. Defines "diary" as a day-to-day record of what interested the "diarist" and as written for "personal reasons". Manuscript diaries are excluded. Some biographical information given, and the notes indicate persons, places and chief subjects. Chronologically arranged by year of first entries—as published. Diarists indexed.

C3   ——————.
British diaries; an annotated bibliography of British diaries written between 1442 and 1942. Berkeley, University of California Press, 1950.

"In general . . . includes diaries written by Englishmen, Scotsmen, Welshmen and Irishmen in the British Isles, in Europe and on the high seas and also the diaries of American and other travelers in the British Isles, so far as they have been published in England and in English." Also includes unpublished diaries. Chronological arrangement; each entry has dates of diary, some biographical data, descriptive notes as to contents—chief subjects, persons, places. Sometimes an evaluative comment is included. A name index compensates for the chronological arrangement.

C4   Ponsonby, Arthur Ponsonby
English diaries; a review of English diaries from the sixteenth to the twentieth century with an introduction on diary writing by Arthur Ponsonby . . . London, Methuen & Co., ltd. [1923].

Cites one hundred and nineteen diarists from all segments of society; biographical information, extensive quotes from the diaries (published and in manuscript) and provides publication data. Diarists are indexed.

C5   ——————.
More English diaries; further reviews of diaries from the sixteenth to the nineteenth century with an introduction on diary reading by Arthur Ponsonby. London, Methuen & Co., ltd. [1927].

Thirty four diaries are reviewed and characterized. As in the previous work the diarists are from all social strata. The location and ownership of the manuscript is indicated and if published all publication data is provided. There is an index of diarists.

C6   ———————.

Scottish and Irish diaries from the sixteenth to the nineteenth century with an introduction by Arthur Ponsonby. London, Methuen & Co., ltd. [1927].

Twenty-six diarists received same format and treatment as in previous publications, however the selection is less representative of the general populace than the *"English Diaries"*.

C7   Matthews, William, comp.

Canadian diaries and autobiographies. Berkeley, University of California Press, 1950.

One thousand two hundred and seventy six diaries and autobiographies, unpublished and published, relating to both British and French Canada. Preface should be read for factors of exclusion. Arranged alphabetically by writer's name, each entry includes biographical data on the writer, time span, brief content notes and bibliographical data.

C8   Duckett, Eleanor Shipley

Women and their letters in the early Middle Ages (by) Eleanor Duckett. (Northampton, Mass., Smith College, 1965).

Factors reviewed that contributed or inhibited the preservation of letters written by women. Actually, a bibliographical essay identifying the letters of those sisters, wives, daughters, lovers and mothers that survived.

C9   Lacretelle, Jacques de

La galerie des amants. Paris, Librarie académique Perin [1963]

Selection of French love letters spanning the period from Heloise and Abelard to Madame de Staël. Bibliography of collected letters appended.

C10 Valentine, Alan Chester, ed.

Fathers to sons: advice without consent. Norman, University of Oklahoma Press, [1963]

Arranged roughly chronologically (1326-1947) each letter has a brief introduction. Bibliographic information regarding the printed source is complemented by a bibliography and name index.

C11 Lee, Vera G., comp.

La vie des lettres, by Vera G. Lee and Joseph D. Gauthier. New York, Van Nostrand Reinhold Co., [1970]

A collection of letters of famous French authors such as Proust, Gide, Stendhal, Saint-Simon, Céline, etc.,—from their works and their lives.

N.B. Published letters can be located through the various library and trade book catalogs as well as bibliographies. The above titles are examples of collections of letters constructed around a central theme, occupation or relationship. Such collections in themselves function as indexes to the literature of letters. Other aids include:

Adolf Bütow, *Die Entwicklung der mittelalterlichen Briefsteller bis zur Mitte des 12. Jahrhunderts* (Greifswald, 1908);

Dorothy Brooke, *Private Letters: Pagan and Christian* (London, 1929);

Hermann Oesterley, *Wegweiser durch die Literatur der Urkundensammlungen* (Berlin, 1885-86), 1, 19-45;

E. Bourgeois et L. André, *Le dix-septième siècle, T. II, Memoires et lettres* (Paris, 1913).

CHARACTER BOOKS, COURTESY BOOKS AND ETIQUETTE BOOKS

D1 Greenough, Chester Noyes, 1874-1938
A bibliography of the Theophrastan character in English, with several portrait characters by . . . prepared for publication by J. Milton French, Cambridge, Harvard University Press, 1947.

Chronologically arranged, 1495-1941, authors are listed alphabetically within year, this bibliography includes separately published characters and character books of both types—Theophrastan and Clarendon. Included also are sketches that border line "character" and other literary forms. Separate indexes of authors, titles and subjects aid use. The "Appendix of titles considered but rejected" provides valuable information

D2 Murphy, Gwendolen
A bibliography of English character—books, 1608-1700. Transactions of the Bibliographical Society, Supplement no. 4, 1925.

Excellent and detailed bibliographic description including library locations and lists of characters. A second section is devoted to "Controversial Characters". An index of Characters and a separate index of Titles aids use.

D3 Newberry Library, Chicago.
A check list of courtesy books in the Newberry library, compiled by Virgil B. Heltzel. Chicago, the Newberry Library, 1942.

The 1536 books published or written before 1775, available in the Newberry Library and meeting the compiler's rather extensive definition of courtesy books. Works of a purely philosophical, technical or scientific nature have been excluded, as well as fiction. Of particular value is the citation of materials usually part of a collection or the complete work of an author alphabetically by author with adequate bibliographic information. Brief notes index includes editors, translations and pseudonyms, warrant titles, titles of anonymous works and those of questionable authorship.

D4 Noyes, Gertrude E.
Bibliography of courtesy and conduct books in seventeenth-century England . . . New Haven, [The Tuttle, Morehouse & Taylor Company] 1937.

Of the 477 titles cited about one fourth are translated in full or in part from the Latin, Spanish, Portuguese, French, German, Greek and Italian. There is one issue of an English fifteenth-century work and 25 are reissues from the sixteenth century. A secondary bibliography of "Discussions of Courtesy Literature" and subject index complete the volume. Each entry has full bibliographical information and appropriate notes concerning translations, contents, etc.

D5   Bobbitt, Mary Reed
A bibliography of etiquette books published in America before 1900. New York, New York Public Library, 1947.
Some 236 titles of books "which give more or less in detail a code based on the conduct of the best people". A distinction is made between courtesy books and those of etiquette. Books on letter-writing, conduct of life, parental advice and the etiquette of a particular activity (weddings, card games, etc.) have been excluded. Title index also cites some essays, lectures, sermons and addresses. Arrangement alphabetically by author with full bibliographical information as well as library locations are provided.

PEDIATRICS, HISTORY OF

E1   National Library of Medicine
Bibliography of the history of medicine, 1964-1969. Bethesda, Maryland, National Library of Medicine.
Includes and supersedes four previous annual bibliographies of the history of medicine and related sciences and professions citing articles, monographs and analytic entries for symposia, congresses and similar publications. All geographic areas and time periods covered. Three sections: 1) "Biographies" including those dealing of famous non-medical persons; 2) "Subject" index headings divided by geographic and/or Chronologic sub-headings; 3) Author listing.

E2   Miller, Genevieve, ed.
Bibliography of the history of medicine of the United States and Canada, 1939-1960. With a historical introd. by W. B. McDaniel, ed. Baltimore, Johns Hopkins Press [1964]
A cumulation of the annual bibliographies reprinted from the Bulletin of the History of Medicine for the years 1939-1960. A classified arrangement with an author index. One third of the work is devoted to biographies.

E3   *Current work in the history of medicine: an international bibliography.* London, The Wellcome Institute of the History of Medicine, v. 1–1954-
A quarterly index to an extensive list of journals; each issue has a subject index and an author index. "No annual or periodic cum-

mulation of these references will be published." An excellent current awareness publication.

E4   *Bulletin of the History of Medicine.* American Association of the history of medicine. Johns Hopkins University. Institute of the history of medicine. Baltimore. 1-, 1933- (1-6 1933-38 as the Institute's bulletin)

Published bimonthly; good current awareness journal.

E5   Schuman, Henry, comp.

From Hammurabi to Gesell, an exhibition of books on the history of pediatrics, from the Trent Collection [Duke University, Medical Center Library]. Washington, Second International Congress on Medical Librarianship, 1963.

A "reasonable representation" of the history of pediatrics, arranged in seven categories. Titles are arranged chronologically within each section, each title "headed" with an identifying or characterizing phrase. Good bibliographic information and history as well as contents notes. Author index compensates for the classified arrangement.

E6   Levinson, Abraham, 1888-

Pioneers of pediatrics. New York, Froben Press, 1943.

Excluding contemporary American and European pediatricians, this brief history begins with a general survey, covers the Graeco-Roman period, the Islamic one and proceeds to the 15th century up to the 20th. Many fine illustrations, good quotes. A five page bibliography contributes to the overall value.

E7   Abt, Arthur F.

Abt-Garrison history of pediatrics. Philadelphia, Saunders, 1965.

Essentially in two sections, the first chapter (172 pages) deals with the history of pediatrics. The second part (Chapters II-XVII) is devoted to "Historic changes and advances in pediatrics during recent times", each chapter focused upon a particular problem, i.e., infectious disease, nutrition, surgery, etc.

E8   Ruhräh, John, comp. & ed.

Pediatrics of the past; an anthology compiled and edited . . . with a foreword by Fielding H. Garrison. New York, Paul B. Hoeber, Inc., 1925.

An excellent source book, spanning the subject from Hippocrates to F. L. Meissner providing translations, sometimes of the complete text, illustrations (54) and full page plates (18). The work of each individual is introduced by a biographical/evaluative description. A bibliography (14 pages), a separate index of names and one for subjects aids the reader.

E9   Peiper, Albrecht

Quellen zur Geschichte der Kinderheilkunde, zusammengestellt, eingeleitet und kommentiert von Albrecht Peiper. Bern, Humber, [1966].

Essentially a biographical dictionary of individuals concerned with children covering a time period of sixteen hundred B.C. to 1856. Each receives about two pages. A bibliography and name index complete the work.

E10 Still, George Frederic, 1868-
The history of pediatrics; the progress of the study of diseases of children up to the end of the XVIIIth century by George Frederic Still . . . London, H. Melford, Oxford University Press, 1931.
Has a special emphasis upon pediatrics in England, but begins his study with the Graeco-Roman period. Many illustrations. Similar format to Ruhräh. Bibliography particularly interesting as it cites inaugural dissertations presented between 1573-1799. A second list cites other pamphlets and dissertations (1729-1797). An index of names and one of subjects complete this section.

E11 Peiper. Albrecht
Chronik der kinderheilkunde 4., erweiterte und umgearbeitete auflage mit 132, zum teil farbigen abbildungen. Leipzig, Veb Georg Thieme, 1966.
This comprehensive overview of all facets of childhood includes illustrations, drawings, excellent bibliographies, name and subject indexes and specialized bibliographies.

ABSTRACTS

F1 *Psychological Abstracts.* v. 1- , Jan. 1927-   . Lancaster, Pa. American Psychological Association, (1927-   ).
Extensive coverage of the international literature of psychology and related areas by providing abstracts, in English, of articles, books and dissertations. The contents of each issue are arranged by broad category. Each issues' author and brief subject index are cumulated in the completed volume.

F2 *Psychological Abstracts, 1927-1960*
Cumulated subject index. Boston, G. K. Hall & Co., 1960.
The subject indexes of the 34 volumes of *Psychological Abstracts* have been cumulated into one alphabetic listing of refined entries. Thus, under one heading, one can find references to the abstracts of books, dissertations and articles on a given subject.

——————, *1st Supplement.* 1961-1965
Boston, G. K. Hall, 1968.
Cumulation of the annual subject indexes of *Psychological Abstracts,* 1961-1965. Format is the same as the basic set.

F3 *Author index to Psychological Index, 1894 to 1935 and Psychological Abstracts, 1927-1958.* Compiled by the Psychology Library, Columbia University. Boston, G. K. Hall & Co., 1960.
A comprehensive alphabetic author index to the psychological literature, periodical and monograph, published between 1894-

1958, and cited in *Psychological Index* and *Psychological Abstracts.*

———————, 1st Supplement.
Boston, G. K. Hall & Co., 1965.
A cumulative author index of Psychological Abstracts, 1959-1963. Unfortunately, it lacks cross references for publications having multiple authors.

F4   *Child development abstracts and bibliography.* v. 1-
Washington, D.C., National Research Council. 1927-
International coverage of periodicals concerned with all aspects of childhood. Classified arrangement includes categories for biology (including infancy), clinical medicine and public health, psychology (development, comparative, experimental), personality, social psychology and sociology, education, psychiatry and clinical psychology. Titles of foreign language articles are translated, each abstract is written in English. Each issue has an author index but only the completed volume has a cumulated author index and a subject index.

F5   *Sociological Abstracts.* v. 1- , Jan.-Oct. 1953. New York.
Classified arrangement of abstracts of books, papers and articles in broad categories, i.e., art, religion, social psychology, social problems and social welfare, the family and socialization, etc. Published six times a year, each issue now has an author and subject index. The annual cumulation has a subject index which is issued about two years after the volume is completed. Like other abstracting services, this one also functions as an index to the literature as well as a means for determining the relevance of the materials under consideration. A decennial index, 1953-1962, assists in the review of the literature.

F6   *Sociology of Education Abstracts.* v. 1- , 1965-   . Liverpool.
Since volume 2, the scope of this service has been expanded to include abstracts of chapters and books as well as journal articles. The premise and objective of this publication is: 1) that sociology can make major contributions to educational problems, and 2) to develop bibliographic access to the literature of the social sciences for those interested in the sociology of education. This dual function is reflected in the two indexes in each issue: 1) Education Study Areas Index; 2) Sociological Study Area Index.

F7   *Research in Education.* v. 1- ; Nov. 1966-
Full bibliographic information and an abstract of usually unpublished material are provided by this monthly publication. "Education" is very broadly defined and a number of the reports, surveys, studies, etc., of interest and value to the sociologist, social historian and interdisciplinary scholar may be identified by use of the subject index available in each issue. *Research in Education* is produced by the Educational Resources Information

Center (ERIC). The documents selected are made available on microfilm or in hard copy. The monthly institutional, author and subject indexes of *Research in Education* cumulate annually; there is also a decennial subject index to ERIC documents: *Complete Guide and Index to ERIC Reports (1960) through December 1969.*

F8   *Abstracts for Social Workers.* v. 1- , 1965-
      Albany. National Association of Social Workers.
      A quarterly abstracting some 200 English Language serial publications as well as books. A classified arrangement of material including such categories as: fields of service, social policy, service methods, profession and history. Each issue has an author index and a subject index which are cumulated annually.

F9   *Historical Abstracts.* 1775-1945. v. 1-   ; March, 1955-
      (Santa Barbara, Calif., etc.) quarterly (irregular)
      Beginning with volume 17, *Historical Abstracts* divided into two sections: Section A—*Modern History Abstracts* covers the period 1775-1914; Section B—*Twentieth Century Abstracts* covers the period 1914 to the present. The arrangement of both publications is classified by general topics then by area or country. There is an annual index and two 5-year indexes of three parts—subject, biographical and author. The annual indexes include in one alphabet author, geographical, biographical and subject entries.

F10   *America, history and life.* v. 1-   ; July 1964-
      (Santa Barbara, Calif.)
      Includes abstracts from about 200 serial publications related to the culture and history of the U.S. (including Atlantic and Pacific dependencies) as well as Canadian history and current affairs. The publications abstracted include those from state and local historical societies, leading journals in the humanities, social sciences and other fields. The classified arrangement includes categories such as North America, Canada, the United States (subdivisions by area and time period), History, the Humanities and Social Sciences. Each issue contains a combined author, geographical, biographical, and subject index. The annual cumulation is superseded by a quinquennial index.

PERIODICAL INDEXES

Use of periodical indexes and abstracting services is imperative as much of the material—research, professional opinion, and current information—published in journals never becomes available in monographic form.

G1   *Bulletin of the Public Affairs Information Service . . .* (New York).
      Public Affairs Information Service, 1915-   , v. 1-

A subject index to periodicals, documents (federal and state), books and multigraphed publications published in English which are primarily concerned with some aspect of the social sciences. Weekly from September to July, fortnightly in August. Annually cumulated. Its extensive subject indexing and diversity of material indexes make it a particularly valuable research resource.

G2 *Social sciences and humanities index.* New York, H. W. Wilson Company, 1907-   , v. 1-

Provides a sophisticated subject and author index to the scholarly, specialized and professional journals as defined by its title. Subject headings have very adequate subdivisions plus excellent "see references". There are also citations to book reviews.

G3 *British humanities index,* 1962-

Supersedes the *Subject index to periodicals.* Subject approach: Annual Volume. See G5.

G4 *Canadian periodical index. Index de périodiques canadiens.* v. 1-   ; Jan. 1948-

A monthly author and subject index to a broad range of Canadian periodicals. Cumulated annually. Cross references from French subject entries to those in English.

G5 *The Subject index to periodicals.* Issued by the Literary Association 1915/16, 1917/19—1962.

Covers about 300 periodicals in the social sciences, humanities, business and important journals from other fields. Quarterly issues with an annual cumulation.

G6 *Cumulated magazine subject index, 1907-1949;* a cumulation of the F. W. Faxon Company's Annual magazine subject index edited by Frederick Winthrop Faxon, Mary E. Bates (and) Anne C. Sutherland. Cumulated by G. K. Hall & Co., Boston, G. K. Hall, 1964.

Designed to complement *Poole's Index,* the *Annual Library Index* and the *Reader's Guide,* it indexed an increasing number (79 to 175) of American, Canadian and English periodicals. Special emphasis given to architecture, travel, geography, education, political science, art, forestry and outdoor life, as well as in depth coverage of the publications of state historical societies.

G7 *Nineteenth century readers' guide to periodical literature, 1890-1899,* with supplementary indexing, 1900-1922; edited by Helen Grant Cushing and Adah V. Morris, New York, H. W. Wilson Co., 1944.

An author, subject and illustrator index to the material in fifty-one periodicals, primarily general and literary although some other fields are covered. Citations are also made to book reviews and there is a title index to poems (13,000), plays, short stories and novels.

N.B. Includes at least 7 periodicals not indexed by *Poole's.*

65

G8 *Poole's index to periodical literature,* by William Frederick Poole
... with the assistance as associate editor of William I. Fletcher
... and the cooperation of the American Library Association and
the Library Association of the United Kingdom. Rev. ed. v. 1,
1802-1887; Supplements: v. 2, 1802-1887; v. 3, 1887-1892; v. 4,
1892-1896; v. 5, 1897-1902; v. 6, 1902-1906.

A subject index to English language periodicals "and only such
of these as are likely to be found in libraries and private collections". A number of scientific and semi-professional publications
have been indexed—at least their general interest articles, but
purely scientific and professional serials including those of botany,
law, medicine, etc. have been excluded. Five year supplements
with increased scope complete this work.

G9 *The Education index.* Jan. 1929-   ; New York, H. W. Wilson Co.

A cumulative author-subject index to English language educational publications—it is primarily an index to periodical literature,
although its scope also includes yearbooks, proceedings, monographs, bulletins and U.S. government documents. Issued monthly,
except for July and August. Comparable publications are the
British Education Index (v. 1- ; Aug. 1954/Nov. 1958-   )
and the *Canadian Education Index* (v. 1- , Jan/March, 1965-   ).

G10 *Writings on American history,* 1902-   (Washington, U. S. Government Printing Office).

Some twelve years in arrears, each volume includes the articles
and books published during a specific year "that has any consid-
erable value for study and research pertaining to the history of
the United States from primitive times to the recent past." Three
sections: 1) devoted to items concerned with the historical profession; 2) the United States, 3) writings concerned with U.S. de-
pendencies, regions, states and territories. The following items are
excluded: newspapers, juvenile books, book reviews, historical
fiction, archeological reports, geneological works without biographical sketches or documents, argumentative articles on statu-
tory law and critical essays on literary topics. Each volume has a
name and place index. There is a cumulative index published for
the years 1902-1940.

G11 *Index Medicus.* n.s. v. 1- , 1960-

Monthly bibliographic listing of references to about 2,200 of
the world's biomedical journals. A separate *Bibliography of Medical Reviews* (which are surveys of the literature) is included as well
as a subject and author index. Separate annual cumulations for
authors and subjects. Predecessors are: *Index medicus* (1879-
1927); *Quarterly cumulative index to current medical literature*
(12 v., 1917-1927); *Quarterly cumulative index medicus* (60 v.,
1927-1956); *Current List of medical literature* (1950-1959). See
also the *National Library of Medicine Catalog.* Books (v. 1- ;

1955-   ), New York Academy of Medicine *Subject Catalog of the Library*.

G12   Grinstein, Alexander.
       The Index of psychoanalytic writings. New York, International Universities Press, 1956-

Vol. 1-5 (nos. 1-37121)
       Updating, correcting and supplementing *Index Psychoanalyticus* this index attempts to cite inclusively the literature by and about psychoanalysts published between 1900 through 1952, books, monographs, articles, in any language, as well as reviews and abstracts from psychoanalytic journals. Alphabetically arranged by author, citations are listed alphabetically by title. Good access is provided by the subject index which is a composite of key words derived from the subject lists of the *Current List of Medical Literature* and *Psychological Abstracts*. The numbers following the subject entries refer to numbered items in the main body of the *Index*.

Vol. 6-9 (nos. 40000-63348)
       A comprehensive bibliography of the psychoanalytic literature published between 1953-1959. Some items published in 1960 are also included and relevant titles published before 1953 but omitted in the first five volumes are included. Foreign language titles are also translated into English.

Vol. 10-14 (nos. 65001-   )
       Comprehensive listing of psychoanalytic literature published between 1960-1969. Based upon the same principles of inclusion as the original set, it does, however, exclude articles in newspapers and popular journals as well as reprints and new editions "unless significantly revised". The arrangement of material is as in the other two series.
       N.B. The reader must check both the original set as well as the supplements to obtain all relevant citations.

G13   U.S. Department of Health, Education and Welfare. Vocational Rehabilitation Administration.
       Psychiatric index for interdisciplinary research: a guide to the literature 1950-1961. Ed. by Richard K. Schermerhorn. Washington, D.C., 1964. 1249 p.
       Limited to the publication period 1950-1961, this bibliography is based upon a selection from 133 journals in psychiatry, psychology, anthropology, sociology, social work, rehabilitation, public health, mental health, medicine, nursing and education. Publications in foreign languages are excluded and books have also been omitted. The "Interdisciplinary" scope of the subject matter excludes abnormal reactions due to neurological or organic damage. The greatest utility of the Index will be in the areas for investigation of conditions directly resulting from functional psychotic dis-

orders, neurotic, psychopathic and character disorders, drug addiction and alcoholism and psychosomatic problems. There are 71 categories in which the articles are arranged alphabetically by author.

G14 Royal Historical Society, London.
Writings on British History, 1901-1933; a bibliography of books and articles on the history of Great Britain from about 400 A.D. to 1914, published during the years 1901-1933 inclusive, with an appendix containing a select list of publications in these years on British history since 1914. London, J. Cape, 1968-   .

Scope differs somewhat from (G15) as it includes entries for society guides and printed or archival materials, the publications of the Stationery Office and cumulative indexes of society transactions. Citations are also limited to relevant foreign books and journal articles published abroad, books published in England and Wales (except those issued by societies) and articles in journals, not issued by societies, published in England and Wales. Each volume is concerned with a specific topic or historical period: v. 1 Auxiliary sciences and general works; v. 2 The Middle Ages 450-1485; v. 3 Tudor and Stuart Periods, 1485-1714; v. 4 The Eighteenth Century, 1714-1815; v. 5, 1815-1914. Each volume has a name index and the Prefatory Note should be read for references to complementary bibliographies and lists of publications excluded.

G15 Royal Historical Society, London.
Writings on British history, 1934-   ; a bibliography of books and articles on the history of Great Britain from about 450 A.D. to 1914, published during the year . . . with an appendix containing a select list of publications . . . on British history since 1914 . . . London, J. Cape, 1937-   .

Attempts to deal "exhaustively" with the yearly production of publications concerned with British history; however, certain aspects of the history of science, literature and the arts are excluded. Items from weekly journals and newspapers, as a rule, have not been included. The bibliography has two parts. Part I— General Works: Auxiliary Sciences, Bibliographies and Indexes, British History in General, Local History and Topography, Wales, Scotland, Ireland, Genealogy and Family History, Collected Biography. Part II—Period Histories subdivided by geographical area or topic, i.e. economic and social history, political history, etc. Each volume has a name and subject index.

G16 *Internationale Bibliographie der Zeitschriftenliteratur,* aus allen Gebieten des Wissens, hrgs. von Otto Zeller, Jahrg. 1- , 1963/64- . Felix Dietrich, 1965-   , v. 1-

More than 7600 periodicals consulted; functions as a subject index to world periodical literature. Subject headings are in German with cross references from English and French forms of.the headings. Continues in a combined form the *Bibliographie der deutschen Zeitschriftenliteratur* and the *Bibliographie der fremd-sprachigen Zeitschriftenliteratur.*

G17 *Bibliographie der deutschen Zeitschriftenliteratur,* mit Einschluss von Sammelwerken . . . 1896-64, Gautzsch b. Leipzig, 1897-64, v. 1-128. Semiannual. *Internationale Bibliographie der Zeitschriftenliteratur, Abt. A.*

Consultation of many alphabets necessary as the semiannual volumes do not cumulate. A comprehensive index to German yearbooks, transactions, composite works and important periodicals, the first volume indexed some 275 magazines, while later volumes covered some 4500. The arrangement is by broad subject with an author index to the subject index. Merged into *Internationale Bibliographie der Zeitschriftenliteratur.*

G18 *Bibliographie der fremdsprachigen Zeitschriftenliteratur.* Répertoire bibliographique international des revues; International index to periodicals 1911-1924, 1925/26-62/64. *Internationale Bibliographie der Zeitschriftenliteratur, Abt. B.*

Useful for locating materials in English and American periodicals as well as Italian, French and other European publications. Indexes over 1400 periodicals and general works. Superseded by *Internationale Bibliographie der Zeitschriftenliteratur.* Because of lack of bibliographic access to French periodicals, this index is particularly important for French material.

ENCYCLOPEDIAS, DICTIONARIES, HANDBOOKS

H1 *International Encyclopedia of the Social Sciences.* D. L. Sill, ed. [New York] Macmillan (1968) 17 v.

The articles, written by scholars from over 30 countries, emphasize the comparative and analytical aspects of the theories, concepts and methodology of the disciplines of Anthropology, Psychology, Geography, Economics, History, Law, Political Science, Psychiatry, Psychology and Statistics. Each article is completed by an extensive and select bibliography. The biographies of some 600 important and key figures in the social sciences are also included. The arrangement of the articles is alphabetic, supplemented by numerous cross references. Volume 17 contains an exhaustive index.

H2 *The Encyclopedia of Education.* Lee D. Ceighton, editor in Chief. [New York] Macmillan & The Free Press (1971-   ) 10 v.

An alphabetic/topical arrangement of more than 1000 articles, usually signed, concerned with all aspects of education—as institution, product and process. Most of the articles have bibliographies appended. The tenth volume contains a directory of contributors and a *Guide to Articles* (an arrangement of related articles under appropriate topics) and a very extensive index.

H3   Ellis, Albert, 1913-   ed.
      The Encyclopedia of Sexual Behavior, edited by Albert Ellis
      and Albert Abarbanel. New and revised second edition. New
      York, Hawthorn Books, 1967.

      The emotional, psychological, legal, sociological, anthropolog-
      ical, geographical and historical aspects of sexuality receive "ex-
      tensive and intensive" coverage in about one hundred authorita-
      tive articles. The significant aspects of the anatomy, biology, and
      psychology of sex as well as love, marriage and the family are
      also examined. Major spokesmen, of international representation,
      from the artistic, literary, professional and scientific disciplines
      are the contributors. The articles are alphabetically arranged by
      their subject. A 39 page index and an analytical guide to the con-
      tents (separate articles are listed under the key concepts of sexual
      behavior) provide maximum utility of this valuable reference
      resource.

H4   *A Dictionary of the Social Sciences,* edited by Julius Gould (and)
      William L. Kolb, New York, Free Press of Glencoe, (1964).

      Social scientists, some 270, define and describe approximately
      one thousand basic social science concepts from the areas of po-
      litical science, social anthropology, economics, social psychology
      and sociology. Both general and accepted scientific usage are pre-
      sented and illustrated by citations and quotations from the liter-
      ature. Consequently, the references to the relevant literature add
      the functions of index and bibliography to this dictionary. Most
      terms have two subsections: A) definitions of the term; B) histori-
      cal background and/or a more detailed discussion. Some entries
      have additional sections which further develop the analytical or
      historical meaning of the word or concept, or they may be con-
      cerned with the specialized meanings of the concept that func-
      tions in the different social sciences.

H5   Hoult, Thomas Ford
      Dictionary of modern sociology. (Tolowe, N.J.) Adams,
      (1969) 408 p.

      Definitions intended to reflect "current concept usage" in so-
      ciological and related literatures. Many examples of usage. Bib-
      liography, quite extensive, of works and authors cited.

H6   American Psychiatric Association. Committee on Public Informa-
      tion.
      A Psychiatric glossary; the meaning of terms most frequently
      used in psychiatry. 3rd ed. Washington (American Psychiatric
      Association) 1969

      Some 800 entries with precise definitions. Some personal
      names included. Utility enhanced by good cross references.

H7   Linzey, Gardner, ed.
      The Handbook of social psychology. Edited by Gardner Lin-

zey and Elliot Aronson. 2nd ed. Reading, Mass., Addison-Wesley Pub. Co. (1968-   ).

Five volumes of forty-five chapters written by 68 authors. The arrangement is: 1) historical introduction and systematic positions; 2) research methods; 3) the individual in a social context; 4) group psychology and phenomena of interaction; and 5) applied social psychology. Each article or chapter has an extensive bibliography. Each volume has its own author index and extensive subject index.

H8   *American handbook of psychiatry.* Silvano Arieti, editor. Editorial board: Kenneth E. Appel (and others) New York, Basic Books, 1959-1966. 3 v.

Divided into 21 parts, 144 articles have been selected and arranged to represent every leading school of thought and major approach. The goal was one of completeness and representation of all points of view with regard to the developments, trends, techniques, problems and prospects of modern psychiatry. Bibliographies, a name index and a detailed subject index are additional features of this handbook.

H9   American Historical Association
      Guide to historical literature. Board of editors: George Frederick Howe, Chairman (and others) assisted by selection editors, a central editor and others. New York, Macmillan, 1961. 962 pp.

Comprehensive approach to the literature of history; classified arrangement by topic (Introduction and General History; General Reference Resources, World History, History of Religions) and geographical/historical area (Ancient Orient, Ancient Greece, Rome, Middle Period in Eurasia and Northern Africa, etc.). Within sections, the following organization has been approximated: Bibliographies, Encyclopedias, Geographies, Gazetters and Atlases, Anthropologic, demographic and linguistic works, printed collections of sources, shorter and longer general histories, histories of periods, areas and topics, Biographies; Government publications; publications of academies, universities and learned societies; Periodicals. Most of the entries have brief annotations. A comprehensive subject and name index complete the volume.

H10   Handlin, Oscar
      Harvard guide to American history, (by) Oscar Handlin (and others). Cambridge, Mass., Belknap Press, 1954

A handbook designed for the general reader, student and scholar, that is both a guide through the body of American historical literature published before 1950 and a manual of historical methodology and resources. Chapters 1-6 comprise sixty-six essays concerned with techniques, materials, sources, aids to research, etc. Appended to each essay is a list of relevant works. The following section is devoted to historical periods. For each period there is a summary of topics presented, citations to general and specific works, both serial and monographic, as well as other sources, maps and bibliographies. Citations are to the best edition of the best works. Often references are made to pages and chapters. Very extensive index included.

DISSERTATIONS, THESES

I1   *American Doctoral Dissertations.* 1936-64-   , Ann Arbor, Michigan, University Microfilms.

A comprehensive listing of dissertations accepted by American and Canadian universities. Arranged by broad subject category, then further subdivided by university and by author. Use is facilitated by a classified table of contents and a cumulated author index. Former title was *Index to American Dissertations* which superseded, in 1955/56, *Doctoral Dissertations accepted by American Universities.*

N.B. This bibliography must be consulted to determine the total academic effort made in a particular discipline as *Dissertation Abstracts International* is only a partial listing.

I2   *Dissertation Abstracts International*

Abstracts of dissertations available on microfilm or as xerographic productions. v. 1- ; Ann Arbor, Michigan, Xerox, University Microfilms, 1938-

Formerly *Dissertation Abstracts,* title change occurred when the scope of this publication was expanded to include dissertations from European universities as well as those of the U.S. and Canada. Abstracts of the dissertations are arranged within broad subject categories. Each monthly issue has a Key Word Index and Author Index with an annual cumulation. Beginning with volume 30, DAI is published in two sections: Humanities (a) and Sciences (b); each one with its own indexes. Abstracts are useful but it should be carefully noted that only about 250 institutions participate in this program.

I3   *Dissertation Abstracts International: Retrospective Index.* Ann Arbor, Michigan, University Microfilms, 1938-1969.

Divided into broad categories, this retrospective index for the first 29 (1938-60) volumes of *Dissertation Abstracts* and *Dissertation Abstracts International* is arranged in nine volumes: 1) Math and Physics; 2) Chemistry; 3) Earth and Life Sciences; 4) Psychology/Sociology/Political Science; 5) Social Sciences; 6) Engineering; 7) Education; 8) Communication/Information/Business/Literature/Fine Arts; 9) Author Index.

Within the appropriate volume, each title is cited by the principle words in the title of the dissertation. Full bibliographic information is provided—title, complete name of author, institution identified, the volume issue and page where the abstract can be found in *Dissertation Abstracts* or *Dissertation Abstracts Interna-*

tional. "How to Use the Index" should be carefully read to use effectively this valuable resource and for information on obtaining dissertations.

N.B. When the name of the author of a dissertation is known, volume 9, the cumulative author index, is particularly useful for the proper bibliographic identification of a dissertation and its rapid location; no small accomplishment when initiating an inter-library loan request since such transactions require accurate and complete information.

Note: Comparable listings of dissertations include: *Index to Theses Accepted for Higher Degrees in the Universities of Great Britain and Ireland,* 1950-   ; France. Direction des biblio-thèques de France. *Catalogue des thèses,* 1884-   ; *Jahresver-zeichnis der Deutschen Hochschulscriften,* 1885-   and *Cana-dian Theses,* 1961-   .

I4   *Masters abstracts: abstracts of selected theses on microfilm.*
Ann Arbor, University Microfilms, Inc., 1962-   .

A classified subject arrangement of abstracts of theses from all fields. Inclusion requires a recommendation by the department head, a representative of or the dean of the graduate school. Full bibliographic information is provided: author's name, title, insti-tution as well as order number. Four quarterly issues with an an-nual cumulative author index and a cumulative subject index. All theses are, of course, available for purchase, either on microfilm or in xerox copy.

I5   *List of doctoral dissertations in history in progress in the United States.* American Historical Association, 1909-

A classified arrangement by broad category, supplemented by a topic index and an author index. A triannial publication that formerly cited dissertations completed. That data is now available in the AHA's *Annual Report.*

N.B. A number of specialized lists of dissertations exist. For example, *Sociology dissertations in American universities,* 1893-1966 (1969); Kuchl, Warren F., *Dissertations in history:* an index to dissertations completed in history departments of the United States and Canadian Universities, 1873-1960 (University of Ken-tucky, 1965), H. West, Earle H., *A Bibliography of Doctoral Re-search on the Negro,* 1933-1966 (1969), etc. Iowa. State Teachers College, Cedar Falls. Bureau of Research. *Masters theses in educa-tion.* 1951/52-

MANUSCRIPTS, SUBJECT COLLECTIONS AND SPECIALIZED RESOURCES

J1   *The National Union Catalog of manuscript collections.* 1959-51-
A continuing series listing those manuscript collections per-manently housed in American repositories "regularly open to

scholars". Up to and including the seventh volume 23,053 collections are described. "Collection" has been broadly defined regarding types of materials. Arrangement is by entry number. The index of names, places, subjects and historical periods provides access through the entry to the relevant collection(s). The Repository Index lists alphabetically the institutions represented and cites the collections in their possession.

J2   U.S. National Historical Publications Commission.
A Guide to archives and manuscripts in the United States. Philip M. Hamer, ed., New Haven, Yale University Press, 1961.

The manuscript and archival holdings of some 1300 depositories in the U.S., Puerto Rico, the Canal Zone and the District of Columbia are described—a statement of field of interest, extent and types of material. Often reference is made to a descriptive journal article about the collection. The arrangement is geographical; alphabetical by state, then by city within the state and then alphabetically by the name of the depositories in the city. The complete address of the institution is included. Use is aided by an extensive name, subject index.

N.B. The "Note on Bibliographical Guides" is a particular value in identifying predecessors to this publication and bibliographic tools for specialized subjects.

Note: There are numerous published book catalogues of manuscripts published by individual libraries and state historical societies. Helpful references may be located in *Manuscripts in public and private collections in the United States,* 1924-   ; *Guide to the Records in the National Archives* (1948) and "Manuscript materials" in Oscar Handlin's, *Harvard Guide to American History,* (1954).

J3   Ricci, Seymour de, 1881-1940
Census of medieval and renaissance manuscripts in the United States and Canada, by Seymour de Ricci, with the assistance of W. J. Wilson. New York, Kraus Reprint Corp., 1961 (1935-40)

Some 6000 manuscripts, written before 1600, in public and private collections, are briefly described with notes on their previous history. Excluded from this "Census" are inscriptions on metal, stone or other hard surfaces, Greek and Latin papyri and all Oriental manuscripts. The arrangement is alphabetical: by state, then by city and finally by library. The third volume contains several indices: General Index of Names, Titles and Headings; Scribes, Illuminators and Cartographers; Inscipits: Gregory Numbers for Greek New Testament Manuscripts; Present Owners; Previous Owners.

—————————. Supplement. Originated by C. U. Fage, continued and edited by W. H. Bond. New York, Bibliographical Society of America, 1962.

J4   American Institute for Research in the Behavioral Sciences
      Handbook of information sources in education and the be-
      havioral sciences, by Jesse L. Gates and James W. Altman. (Wash-
      ington) U.S. Dept. of Health, Education and Welfare, Office of
      Education, Bureau of Research, 1968.
         Emphasis is upon supplemental information resources to li-
      braries, periodicals and books such as: Guides and directories;
      Multi-disciplinary information centers; Data repositories; Indexing
      and abstracting services; and Specialized information centers.
      There is a brief subject index.

J5   McDonald, Donna, comp. & ed.
      *Directory of historical societies and agencies in the United
      States and Canada,* 1973-1974. A Joint Publication of the Ameri-
      can Association for State and Local History, Nashville, Tenn. and
      Inforonics, Inc., Maynard, Mass., 1972.
         About 5000 organizations are listed. A geographical arrange-
      ment by state or province, then by city or town. Each entry in-
      cludes name, mailing address, telephone number, year founded,
      name of paid or elected officer, number of members, number of
      staff and cites periodical publications. Major programs supported
      by the society are indicated. A title index provides rapid access.

J6   Ash, Lee, 1917-   comp.
      *Subject collections; a guide to special book collections and
      subject emphasis as reported by university, college, public and
      special libraries in the United States and Canada,* compiled by
      Lee Ash and Denis Lorenz. 3rd ed., rev. & enl., New York, R. R.
      Bowker Company, 1966-
         An alphabetic subject arrangement with good cross references,
      some 35 to 40,000 references are made to special collections.
      Within subject the arrangement is by state, then by city and al-
      phabetically by the name of the library. Full address is given plus
      brief description of the extent and nature of the material.
         Excluded from this directory are local history collections. The
      listings are not complete for academic departmental libraries,
      medical, law or nursing libraries.

J7   Aslib
      Aslib directory, edited by J. Wilson. London, Aslib, 1968-
      Published by the Association of Special Libraries and Information
      Bureau since 1928.
         Volume One: Information sources in science, technology, and
      commerce.
         Volume Two includes sources of information on the social sci-
      ences, the humanities and medicine as well as history, geography,
      law, sports, theology and the arts. The arrangement is geographi-
      cal-alphabetical by postal town. Each entry includes the name,
      address, a brief description of the purpose of the organization,

scope of information available, approximate size of collection, and publications. The name index includes those of the organization, any named special collection or any other noted material. The subject index is extensive with lavish cross references.

J8   Lewanski, Richard Casimir, 1918-
Subject collections in European libraries; a directory and bibliographical guide. Compiled by Richard C. Lewanskii. (New York) R. R. Bowker Co., 1965.

The special collections of about 6000 libraries are indexed according to the Dewey Decimal Classification. Within each classification the sequence is: country, city within that country, followed by the name of the library. For each institution the extent of information varies but usually includes the address, the name of the special collection, the individual in charge, the extent of and type of materials and the restrictions involved. The inclusion of a short version of the Dewey Decimal Classification and a subject index facilitates use.

J9   *Human Relations Area Files*
755 Prospect Street, New Haven, Connecticut, Box 2054 Yale Station 06520

HRAF is a highly developed information retrieval system providing rapid access to substantive and descriptive rather than theoretical data on primarily non-western cultures, many of them non-literate. As of 1969, files had been established for 286 societies; the goal is 400. At that time the total number of sources in the files was 4,112, with 458,207 text pages generating a total of an estimated 2,737,000 file slips. The sources are books, articles or manuscripts that have been evaluated by specialists. The decision to include the document in the files requires it to be annotated according to the 710 cultural and natural categories. According to the number of categories indicated on a page, that page is reproduced that number of times and each copy is filed behind its proper category guide card, thus all materials on one subject or aspect of a subject are placed in one file. Due to problems of defining categories the efficient and effective utility of HRAF requires the use of the *Outline of Cultural Materials* (OCM) and the *Outline of World Cultures* (OWC).

Physically, the Files are in two formats—a paper edition or on microfilm cards—which has extended their availability. Originally designed to serve anthropology and the related social sciences, students and scholars from all the social sciences, the arts, botany, zoology and law have found the Files useful. The researcher in Childhood history may find the files on the two historical societies useful—Imperial Rome (OWCE 19) and Historical Massachusetts (OWC—NL7).

NEWSPAPERS

K1   *New York Times Index to microfilm for the years 1851-1873- .*
New York Times Index; a master key to all newspapers. v. 1- ,
Jan./Mar., 1913-   , New York, The New York Times.

An excellent index giving exact references to date, page and
column. Fine use of cross references to names and related topics.
Particularly useful in determining the date of passage of federal
and state legislation and biographical material, especially in the
newspaper obituary section. Reviews of books are listed under
the entry "Book Reviews". Because the microfilm edition is retrospective to 1851, the index may serve as an independent reference
to dates and events as well as providing a guide to the historical
development of trends, attitudes, and institutions.

K2   *The Official Index to the Times. Index to the Times.* Jan./June
1906-

Initially annual subject and name index. In 1914 six-month indexes available and beginning in 1965, index covers a period of
two months. Book reviews and notices are listed under the subject
heading "Book Reviews".

K3   The Times, London
Palmer's index to the Times Newspaper.

A quarterly subject and name index that does not cumulate,
covering the period 1790-1939.

Note: While a number of published indexes (Wall Street Journal
index, the Virginia Gazette index, 1736-1780, etc.) exist, often
others are available in a variety of forms either in the newspaper
offices or in the public library of the place of publication. For
topics and events of more than local interest, the index to the
New York Times or that of the Times can be used as a guide to
locating materials in other newspapers.

K4   U.S. Library of Congress. Union Catalog Division.
Newspapers on Microfilm. 1st- ed. 1948-

The 6th edition contains approximately 21,700 entries for
17,000 domestic newspapers and 4,600 foreign, representing all
fifty states, America, Samoa, Guam, Okinawa, Puerto Rico and
the Virgin Islands and 136 countries.

The list is geographical, by state and city, province and city for
Canada and the French West Indies. For other countries it is
simply by city.

Entries indicated periodicity, inclusive publication dates, location of negative microfilm and the extent of files available. When
possible, an effort has been made to indicate location of positive
microfilm files.

K5   *American newspapers 1821-1936, a union list of files available in
the United States and Canada,* edited by Winifred Gregory under

the auspices of the Bibliographical Society . . . New York, W. H. Wilson Co., 1937.

The distinction between newspapers and periodicals during this time period is difficult. Consequently titles that appeared in the *Union List of Serials* and the *List of Serial Publications of Foreign Governments* have been excluded as well as those publications of primary interest to limited groups, i.e., labor unions, fraternal lodges, religious denominations, etc.

The arrangement is alphabetic by state or province (Canada is a separate section) and then city. Under city, the newspapers are arranged alphabetically by the first important word, excluding the name of the town, days of the week, and such designations as daily, weekly, etc.

Information provided includes, when possible, inclusive date of publication and citations for those institutions having a file of the newspaper and the extent of that file.

Note: Other examples of types of locating and identification sources are: *Latin American Newspapers in the United States Libraries;* a union list (1968, 1969); Brown, Warren Henry, 1905- , *Checklist of Negro Newspapers in the United States* (1827-1946) Jefferson City, Mo., School of Journalism, Lincoln University, 1946, Duke University, Durham, N.C. Library, *A Checklist of United States' Newspapers (and weekly before 1900) in the General Library,* compiled by Mary Wescott and Allene Ramage, Durham, N.C., Duke University 1921-37. 6 v.

INDEX